Organizing Love in Church

Tim Adeney and Stuart Heath

Organizing Love in Church

Published by:
Gospel Groundwork Pty Ltd
PO Box 309
SUMMER HILL NSW 2130
AUSTRALIA
www.gospelgroundwork.com
training@gospelgroundwork.com

 160303

ISBN 978-1-922110-16-9

Cover design by Stan de Wijs (projectstan.com). Front cover illustration by Sébastien Drouyer (isaxar.com). Back cover illustration by Freepik (freepik.com).

Contents

Overview

This is a book about how to organize God's people so that they're better able to love him and love their neighbours. In other words, it's about social architecture that promotes love.

Most of us are familiar with architecture as a profession. If you hope a building is going to serve some useful purpose and it's going to last a long time, you probably can't 'just build it': it needs to be designed, or architected. Similarly, we think that as we seek to build a Christian community, we probably won't 'just love': we'll have to design conditions that make it easier for our church members to love God, his people, and his world.

We've outlined our rationale and a basic blueprint for social architecture in churches in three chapters:

1. The New Testament pictures church as a community of love: God loves his people and his world; his people love God and one another; together, God's people extend his love to the world.
2. For churches to love in this way, they require *organization.* But the way many of our churches are currently organized doesn't necessarily facilitate love; in fact, it may make it harder.

3. There's no precise formula for social architecture, but we make some concrete suggestions that might be useful for promoting love in a range of churches.

Our focus here is quite narrow, and it's worth clarifying what this book is *not*. It's not a complete doctrine of church. Rather, we've only drawn on our view of church to the extent that it's required to talk about social architecture. So this book should be useful to those with a quite different ecclesiology from ours, as long as their view includes the people of God loving one another and loving unbelievers together.

This book is also not intended to be equally useful for all Christians: it's primarily written for those who lead God's people in some way. All believers are responsible for how they faithfully follow Jesus, but only leaders are responsible for creating conditions in which *others* follow Jesus.[1] So, for example, while almost everyone is able to offer hospitality, only those responsible for a group can really help everyone develop a culture of hospitality. And while everyone needs to find ways of doing good within their context, only a few have the opportunity to overhaul their context.

So it's this group of leaders — those who've been given responsibility to oversee a group of Christians living out their discipleship together — that we particularly hope this book will help.

---

[1] The idea and language of 'creating conditions' come from Andrew Cameron.

1. Love in church: what we're all aiming for

A story of a church's love

Here's the story of Magda,[2] a friend of ours who came to Christ about three years ago.

She was a recently-separated single mum who was looking for friends in her neighbourhood. She joined a playgroup run by a local church. A few of the women from that playgroup became her friends. They began to love her in a range of ways, for example: helping her negotiate the court system as she worked through the divorce and custody; babysitting for her so that she could have a break (both in regular timeslots and spontaneously); helping her find paid work. Magda also got to see how these Christian women loved one another in their church community.

As part of these friendships, there were opportunities for a number of conversations about Jesus. Magda had had some church experience as a child, which had left her with the impression that Christianity was irrelevant and hypocritical.

[2] Throughout this book, names have been changed.

But these women who were serving her cut across her prejudice. Eventually, she decided she wanted to properly investigate Jesus. She asked her friends a lot more questions. She joined a Bible study and later came to Sunday gatherings. A few months later, she committed her life to Christ.

Since then, Magda's grown in Christ in various ways. She's had to think through what it means to follow Jesus in her difficult circumstances as a single mum (who also does part-time paid work; who shares custody but has a difficult relationship with her ex; who may one day like to remarry, and so on). She's grown in virtues like patience and self-control. She's joined in the life of the church and is involved in the various ways that the church is a blessing to its members and a blessing to the surrounding community.

In a sense, there's nothing remarkable about this story — at least, not from the human perspective. There's no astounding act of heroism or self-sacrifice; there are just everyday activities that God has used miraculously to bring someone from death to life and from enmity to adoption.

And yet in many of our churches, this sort of story is sadly rare: we seldom see new people come to know Jesus for the first time; we're not sure we can see much concrete growth in godliness in ourselves or in other church members. We'd love to see that change.

A process of love in church

Being included in Christ and growing like him are the work of God's Spirit, but God often accomplishes these things through the ordinary initiatives of his people. If we're not seeing our church grow in love for God, his people, and his world, it's possible that we're doing all the right things, but God's just not blessing our efforts. But where there's a lack of fruit, it's at least worth asking whether the vine needs tending — whether what we're doing is in fact what God has asked us to do, or whether there are things we've inadvertently overlooked. Because our hope is that when God blesses, he blesses *through* us rather than *in spite of* us.

We think Magda's story exemplifies some of the means God uses to see love flourish among his people. There are some patterns in how a church reaches new people (mission),[3] how it includes them (fellowship), and how it helps them grow as followers of Jesus (discipleship). As we describe these patterns, we think there emerges a kind of *process* for how churches express love. We're not articulating this process to be prescriptive ("You must do this"), but rather descriptive ("This is how things tend to happen — these are some ways that God seems customarily to work"). This doesn't mean that every expression of love in our church can be captured by a process, or that somehow the value of our love depends on a process. But we feel that Magda's story exemplifies five elements of mission, fellowship, and discipleship. Perhaps enumerating these can help diagnose some of the weaknesses in our own church culture.

As we describe these five elements of love, it's worth asking:

---

[3] We acknowledge that this is a loose use of the term, which has at its heart the idea of being 'sent', and which is often reserved more for love-by-word than love-by-deed.

- Can we explain why this element is important (either by reference to the Bible or by our observation of the world)?
- Does this element of love consistently appear in either our church culture or the wider society?
- If it's not present in the wider society, does the church help bring it about?

A process for mission

Anecdotally, people who haven't grown up in Christian homes come to know Jesus in a range of ways, but in our experience Magda's story is fairly typical. We might represent it diagrammatically like this:

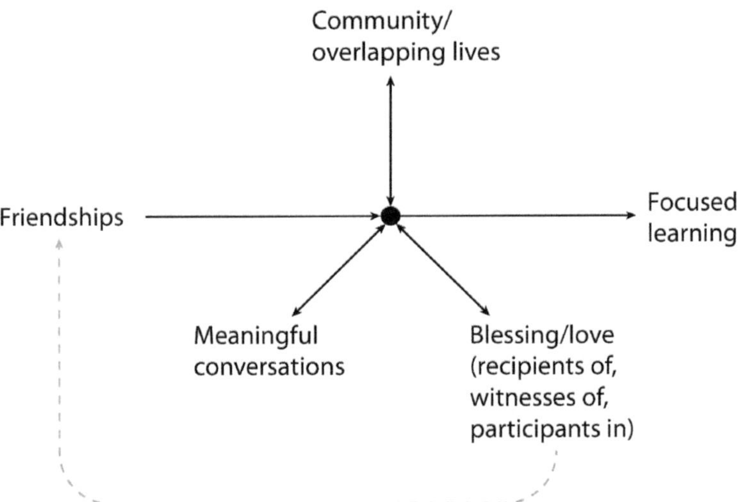

Friendships

We know that Sunday church attendance is declining in the West, and regular churchgoers are now in the minority in most countries.[4] So if the majority of our neighbours are going to encounter Jesus, it's likely to be through a Christian friend. In friendships, we get to love one another in a range of ways; and so over time, Christian friends will be able to bear witness to Jesus in both word and deed. In no particular order, a Christian might introduce their non-Christian friend to Jesus through conversations, community, and blessing.

MEANINGFUL CONVERSATIONS

Many of us — and perhaps particularly men — struggle to have meaningful conversations on any topic (let alone things directly related to Jesus). This normally requires a certain level of friendship: that is, we need to be sure that people love us in a range of ways before we're prepared to be vulnerable with them and discuss something we care about. For most people, it takes time to develop a friendship to the point of being able to explore 'spiritual matters'. And even when we do get to talk about Jesus with our non-Christian friends, we often don't get to explain the whole gospel in one go.

COMMUNITY AND OVERLAPPING LIVES

Our hope is that our non-Christian friends get to meet other Christians. As they see the way that Christians love one another, they'll know that we're Jesus' disciples (John 13:34–35). As a community, we get to bear witness to Jesus in ways that an individual believer can't. And if I'm not a very gifted

---

[4] In Australia, the NCLS say only 20% attend regularly; half of these are Roman Catholic (http://www.ncls.org.au/default.aspx?sitemapid=23).

evangelist, there might be someone else in my community who can explain the gospel to my friend more clearly than I can.

Blessing or love

Both individually and as a community, we should seek to bless or do good to those around us. Sometimes this will be through an activity we organize ourselves (e.g. giving ESL lessons or cleaning up an elderly neighbour's garden); sometimes it will be through us getting involved in what someone else is doing (e.g. volunteering at a drop-in centre run by the local government). As we do these things, our neighbours and friends are both *recipients* of blessing and *witnesses* of blessing. We may also find opportunities for them to be *participants* in blessing others with us — that is, we might invite our unbelieving friends to join us in doing good to others. Our friends with a strong sense of social justice or community spirit would love to get involved in these activities; over time, we might have opportunities to explain to them why we like to serve our neighbours. (The dotted arrow coming out of this box in the diagram reminds us that, as in Magda's case, friendships sometimes start via an event the church runs — what below we'll call a 'love the many' activity.)

Focused learning

Overall, the process we've outlined assumes that, via the Christian community, our friends and neighbours need to see and hear that belonging to Jesus is good news. If this has happened and the Holy Spirit is at work in our friends, they'll probably need a period of focused learning or intentional study before they properly understand and welcome the gospel. This might simply be asking a lot of questions; it might involve joining a Bible study or coming to church gatherings or evangelistic events; it may include reading books, downloading talks, and so on.

A process for fellowship and discipleship

When we describe how people grow in Christlikeness, we find that all the same elements are required. The difference is that they're all present all at once — it's not so much a progression through time:

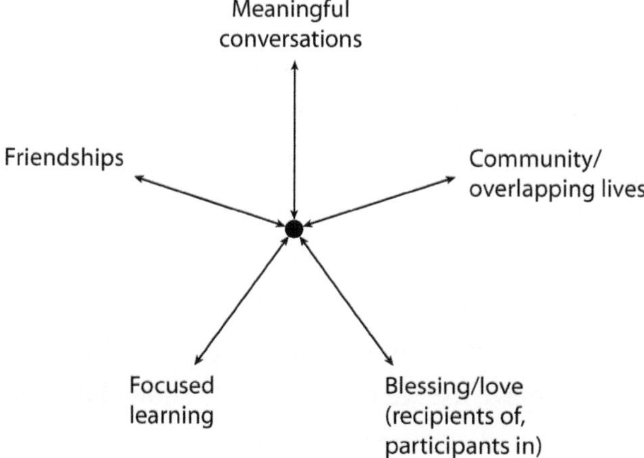

Friendships

Modelling and teaching godliness are most likely to take place in the context of 'iron-sharpening-iron' friendships. Some of these friendships should be intergenerational, so that the older can teach the younger.

Meaningful conversations

Christian friendships will of course involve meaningful conversations, including conversations about Jesus. It's here that we get to speak the truth to one another in love; to teach, rebuke, correct, and train in righteousness; to encourage one another daily, as long as it's called "Today," so that none of us may be hardened by sin's deceitfulness. It's hard for this sort of conversation to take place in most Bible study groups; it's near-impossible in a mixed-gender group. We'll need other contexts. (And as an aside, it's unlikely that we'll be better at talking about important issues with unbelievers than we are with believers.)

Community and overlapping lives

God calls us to himself as individuals, but he also calls us into a family of believers. So without a faithful Christian community, we can't properly display the glorious work of God among us. We can't show that God has broken down dividing walls of hostility to make us one in Christ; we can't use our gifts for the common good; we can't be kind and compassionate to one another, forgiving each other, just as in Christ God forgave us; we can't properly show the world that Jesus' reign is good and not tyrannical.

Blessing or love

The Christian community should be a blessing beyond itself, but it should also be a blessing to be in (Galatians 6:10) — the distinctive thing about us as Jesus' people is that we love God and love one another.

Focused learning

Proper discipleship involves hard thought about the details of everyday life. We need a robust evangelical ethic — a good theology of God's character, of the nature of the world (it's created good; it's fallen; its redemption has been inaugurated; it's awaiting full restoration), and of the various spheres in which we're called to be godly — marriage, parenting, work, wealth, political engagement, evangelism, and so on. We can learn these things in the normal course of reading through Scripture, as well as through expository sermons and inductive Bible studies. But we'll also require systematic study of these aspects of godliness. This is because if you've never thought about a particular topic ("What does the Bible say about marriage?" or "What does the Bible say about the kind of career I should pursue?"), it's very hard to arrive yourself at a conclusion via an inductive Bible study. It's much easier to learn when someone presents you with a thesis up front: you can then discuss it and dissect it, holding it up to the bar of Scripture and seeing if it's applicable in your real, God-given circumstances.

• • •

Although we started by articulating a process, it's worth noting that the individual elements can and should be present regardless of whether they're part of a process. That is, we should expect a godly church to be marked by love in word and deed. This love doesn't spring just from a process, but from the Biblical story of God's love: God shows the world his love throughout history and supremely through the death and resurrection of Jesus Christ; he in turn calls us to love him, his people, and his world. The point of the process is simply to help us see some typical ways that God's people grow in love. So if we find that our church isn't displaying the kind of love we'd like, thinking through the elements of this process might help diagnose where the problem lies.

From what we've said here, it should be clear that we think friendships are key to creating communities of mutual and sacrificial love. This is an important enough idea (and a neglected enough practice) to warrant some further explanation.

Excursus: Love and friendship

Christians get to love one another through friendships

Growing more Christlike requires a change in both beliefs and behaviour. Scripture is a pre-eminent gift to bring about this change: the Bible is where God tells us who he is, what his world is like, what extraordinary things he's done for us, and how we should respond to him. The Holy Spirit makes our hearts and minds alive to God and his self-revelation so that we respond to him in repentance, faith, gratitude, love, obedience, and worship.

But Scripture isn't *the only* gift that equips us for every good work, and by itself, it may not be enough: it's possible to know everything that Scripture says without knowing how to actually love or live wisely (Mark 7:1–23; cf. John 5:35–39).[5] Of

---

[5] The problem in these cases appears to be a 'heart issue'. But we can equally imagine, say, regenerate and enthusiastic Bible scholars who simply don't know how to disciple their family-members or manage a household. In no way should this be construed as an attack on the Reformation principle of *sola Scriptura* or the sufficiency of Scripture (to which we wholeheartedly subscribe). For more on this, see chapters 7–8, 'Bringing life to the Scriptures', in the Groundwork Everyday course *Love and Wisdom.*

course, understanding Scripture is absolutely *necessary*: you can't be trained in righteousness *without* it. But for fellowship and discipleship in Christian community, God has also given us the necessary gift of good-quality friendships.

We can see such friendships and their fruit in the New Testament church. In the Great Commission (Matthew 28:18–20), Jesus says, "Go and make disciples of all nations, baptizing them in the name of the Father and of the Son and of the Holy Spirit, and teaching them to obey everything I have commanded you." As the first disciples obey Jesus' command — as they go and make disciples, teaching them to obey Jesus — they pass on not just a set of theological concepts, but also a way of life. They pass on both beliefs and behaviours. They teach churches with words (all New Testament letters include sections on specific aspects of godliness for the recipients); they also teach through godly modelling. Paul makes a lot of this, repeatedly highlighting the value of learning from and imitating others' godly lives (e.g. 1 Corinthians 4:17; 11:1; Ephesians 4:20–21; 2 Timothy 3:10).

So as Paul writes instructions to his protégés, Timothy and Titus, he encourages them to teach not just the Scriptures (1 Timothy 4:13), but godliness in all of life. He reminds them that God has called them to a holy life (2 Timothy 1:9); he points to the example he and others have set for them (e.g. 2 Timothy 3:10–14); he charges them to watch both their life and doctrine closely (1 Timothy 4:16), so that they can also teach godliness through modelling (1 Timothy 4:12; Titus 2:7–8).

It's very hard for modelling and teaching to happen if we don't have any iron-sharpening-iron friendships. It's as we spend time together, 'life on life', that we benefit from one another's gifts, learn from one another's strengths, and notice one another's sinful blindspots. If the extent of our friendship is a discussion at morning tea on Sundays, I'll never learn from how you treat your spouse and children (or notice if you have a tendency to snap at them). And where I need to hear words of correction or rebuke from you, it'll be easier for me to trust that you're speaking the truth in love if it's in the context of a friendship where you love me in many ways.

Christians get to love their neighbours together through friendships

So good-quality friendships can contribute to fellowship and discipleship. They also have a key role in mission. As noted, because of declining church attendance, many Westerners' first meaningful exposure to Jesus will come through a friend. The reasons people don't come to church will vary from place to place.[6] But this much is clear: if we're going to lead new people to Christ, we can't just wait for them to walk into our church building on a Sunday.[7]

Far more likely, they'll need first to *see* how Jesus is

---

[6] In our Australian setting, many of our neighbours are either antagonistic (27%) or apathetic (37%) towards church (http://www.ncls.org.au/default.aspx?sitemapid=2337). A McCrindle survey suggests that the main reason for non-attendance, cited by 47% of respondents, is that "It's irrelevant to my life." (http://blog.mccrindle.com.au/the-mccrindle-blog/church_attendance_in_australia_infographic).

[7] Of course, if people *do* walk in, then praise Jesus. Let's love them properly. But that can't be our primary strategy for promoting and proclaiming Jesus.

relevant to our day-to-day lives. This is the expectation of the New Testament: when we lead distinctive lives of love, it'll "make the teaching about God our Saviour attractive" (Titus 2:1–10; cf. 1 Peter 2:1–12). If we show how good it is to follow Jesus — if we show what kind of king he is — it makes sense that people might want to ask questions about who he is and what it means to live for him.[8]

Again, what we're describing is the everyday love of friendship: things like sharing meals, going to movies, babysitting for one another, helping to move house or clean up a garden, sharing advice, being there in the midst of heartache or bereavement.

People who don't know Jesus might experience this sort of love in a Christian community both by being direct beneficiaries of it (i.e. they're loved by Christian friends) and by witnessing it (i.e. they see Christians loving one another). In either case, this implies that there's a certain amount of overlap in our circles of Christian and non-Christian friends. If an individual Christian loves their non-Christian friend, they can easily be written off as an eccentric. But if a non-Christian person sees and benefits from the love of a whole community, it's a much more powerful witness.

In addition, friendship is often the best context for evangelism, for several reasons. First, if we speak about Jesus in the context of a loving relationship, it's clear that we're

---

[8] This might be particularly important for those of our friends who've had *negative* experience of church or Christians (including, say, Aboriginal and Torres Strait Islander people and members of the LGBTQ community).

speaking *out of love* (rather than trying to impose our beliefs or to rack up another convert). Second, our gospel speech is likely to be more intelligible and incisive. We'll know which particular false ideas our friend has about God, which particular idols they're attracted to, which particular desires drive their behaviour. In short, we'll know how the gospel is good news *for them*: how Jesus speaks both a word of judgment and a word of hope *into their real circumstances.* (And yes, of course we'll need to tell them about their desperate need for forgiveness: that they stand condemned and deserving of God's wrath, and yet Jesus has died to pay their penalty for them. But this isn't *the only* thing they need to know and it may not be *the first* thing we get to tell them.)

This is what happened with Magda: she had a number of conversations with several people over a few months, before engaging in a more intentional and intensive investigation of Christian claims.

So if we feel like our church isn't doing so well in the areas of fellowship, discipleship, and mission, one question to ask is whether we're promoting the friendships in which these activities normally take place.[9] Sometimes friendships form because we just 'click' with someone; this usually happens when the two of us are quite alike. But we can also become friends over time as we work together on common tasks; in this case, we can become friends with people who are quite

---

[9] This isn't to say that we try to mechanically foster friendship *in order* to promote discipleship and mission: friendships are good in themselves and should be entered into for their own sake.

different from us. This latter path to friendship —of co-operating on tasks over time — is important among a diverse group of people (like a church), as it can help avoid creating cliques or leaving some people excluded. (In chapter 3, we make some concrete suggestions for ways to promote friendships in church.)

Of course, friendship doesn't only belong in church, and believers' relationships outside church will shape both them as individuals and the church community to which they belong. So although we're primarily concerned with love in *church* in this book, to properly describe what we're envisioning, we need to take a step back and make a few more general observations about love in every part of life.

Love in every part of life

> [Jesus said], "'Love the Lord your God with all your heart and with all your soul and with all your mind.' This is the first and greatest commandment. And the second is like it: 'Love your neighbour as yourself.' All the Law and the Prophets hang on these two commandments."
> (Matthew 22:37–40)

> Dear friends, let us love one another, for love comes from God. Everyone who loves has been born of God and knows God. Whoever does not love does not know God, because God is love. This is how God showed his love among us: He sent his one and only Son into the world that we might live through him. This is love: not that we loved God, but that he loved us and sent his Son as an atoning sacrifice for our sins. Dear friends, since God so loved us, we also ought to love one another.
> (1 John 4:7–11)

'Love' is the great summary of the Christian life. In his grace — his unmerited kindness — God has loved us; he now calls us to love him and to love the things that he loves. We can only answer this call because God mercifully gives us a new life in Christ and he comes to dwell among us by his Spirit. This new life implies a new way of living: we're devoted to doing good (Titus 3:8); we put off sin and put on righteousness in every area of life — our work, our families, our friendships, and so on (e.g. Colossians 3:1–4:1). And so over time, we grow to maturity — we grow to be more like Jesus.[10]

This vision of Christian maturity is all-encompassing: whole-of-life discipleship is what we pray for, what we strive for, and what we encourage one another towards. But our temptation can be to locate Christian maturity just in activities related to *church* — that is, to think that a mature Christian is merely someone who knows how to do quiet times, how to run a weekly Bible study, how to teach a Scripture class, how to welcome newcomers on Sundays, and how to give a potted gospel presentation. (Our training programmes are likely to show where our emphasis lies.) Without question, it's good to be godly and skilled in church activities. But it's not sufficient: there's no corner of my life left unchanged by the new identity God has given me in Christ, and there's no corner of creation outside God's sovereignty or care. Everything I do, I do for him. In what follows, we outline a few key aspects of the love that we hope the people of God display.

---

[10] For more on the connection between the gospel, grace, and godliness, see the Groundwork Everyday course *Love and Wisdom*, especially chapters 1 and 2.

Love involves both words and deeds

We express our love in both words and deeds. We think it's important to highlight both of these because it seems it's easy to forget one or the other. Some churches have underplayed or even abandoned loving speech, such as the clear teaching of Scripture and the proclamation of the gospel. In our circles, however, we seem more tempted towards the error of downplaying lives of love and righteousness — the error of neglecting good deeds. There may be several reasons for this: perhaps we fear becoming like those churches that have pursued the 'social gospel'; maybe we worry that any talk of good works will encourage people towards trusting in their own efforts for their salvation; perhaps we hope that if we just exegete the text of Scripture correctly, the Holy Spirit will do the rest and grow the church to maturity. But God's consistent call in the Bible is for his faithful people to love others — to do concrete good to them — in a variety of ways (see, for example, John 15:13; 1 Corinthians 13:4–7; Colossians 3:12–17; 1 Peter 4:8–10; 1 John 3:17–18).[11]

There's no question that false teaching poisons a church and dishonours God. But so too does 'false living' — whether it's the false living of flagrant sin, or the false living of a quiet adherence to the middle-class values of the surrounding culture. This dishonours God in itself, but it also clouds the gospel for the watching world. If our church has orthodox

[11] This isn't the *only* way the Bible uses the word 'love'. Nor should we think that love is merely cold or calculating: we hope that doing good will also rouse our affections. But we think that when Jesus says, "Love your neighbour," it involves *at least* good words and good actions.

teaching but unchanged lives, we communicate two contradictory messages: on the one hand, we *say* that following Jesus is the most important thing in the world; on the other, we *show* that following Jesus makes little or no difference. An unbeliever who comes into contact with such a church may well hear the latter message more loudly.

So we think that churches — and mature Christians — should display both faithful words and faithful lives. God by grace is at work in Christians to transform both our beliefs and our behaviour. Our minds are renewed as the Spirit brings light to God's word (Romans 12:1–2); our character, words, and deeds display the Spiritual fruit of joy, peace, forbearance, kindness, goodness, faithfulness, gentleness, and self-control (Galatians 5:22–23). This is what it means to be a 'disciple' or 'follower': if we follow Jesus, we seek to live like him, to lead distinctive lives of love in all that God's called us to — as spouses, children, parents, friends, stewards, workers, church members, coaches, citizens, and much more besides.

Love is directed towards both believers and unbelievers

And as disciples, we're called to love both the church and the world, both 'insiders' and 'outsiders':

> Let us not become weary in doing good, for at the proper time we will reap a harvest if we do not give up. Therefore, as we have opportunity, let us do good to all people, especially to those who belong to the family of believers. (Galatians 6:9–10)

As a shorthand for this, we might describe church as both a blessing to be in and a blessing beyond itself. By saying a church is a blessing to be in, we're covering what's often meant by 'fellowship' (i.e. including people in the church's love and forming loving partnerships between churches) and 'discipleship' (i.e. growing believers to maturity).[12] When we say church is a blessing beyond itself, we're describing 'mission' in the broadest sense (i.e. loving outsiders with both words and deeds).

As with words and deeds, we face the the temptation to prioritize loving *either* church members *or* those who don't know Jesus, or perhaps to try to achieve a balance between them. The problem with these metaphors of 'priority' and 'balance' is that they pit love for the church and love for the world as rivals, as if they're inevitably competing for our time and energy. But these two directions of love aren't opposed to one other; rather, they work together and reinforce each other. Therefore both need to be done well, or neither will be done well.

Consider a church that's weak at loving outsiders. In this case, whatever love you have for one another is very different from the love that Jesus has for others. His love welcomes outsiders: he left the 99 and went looking for the one; he loved sinners, tax collectors, and Samaritans. He died for the world while we were still his enemies. And now he calls on us to do good to all people as we have opportunity.

---

[12] We're conscious that we haven't included 'worship' here. This silence shouldn't be seen as particularly significant: we understand the language of 'worship' can refer *both* to our whole lives (i.e. every moment of our lives is a spiritual sacrifice; Romans 12:1) *and* to more specific activities of the assembled people of God (such as prayer, praise, word, and sacrament). This isn't the place to try to convince anyone of a particular view of worship, but we hope that what we say about fellowship, discipleship, and mission can serve *regardless* of what you think about worship.

At a practical level, a church which has no outsiders to bless and no effective external mission to share in will likely implode in infighting and irrelevance. If you always ask the question (even implicitly), "What's good for my club and my culture?", in the end you'll be unable to welcome even your own children. Because children are outsiders born inside: they may belong to your family and to your church, but they also belong to a different culture. And when you refuse to bless other cultures around you, in the end you'll refuse to bless the culture of your own children. We all know the stereotype of the church which has clung not just to orthodox confessions but also to traditional practices and routines in such a way that it's effectively refused to welcome outsiders. Such churches often find that they lose their own children as well: eventually they get the message the church has been sending: "You're not welcome here."

Similarly, a church that's weak at loving existing members has grim prospects. If you're great at serving outsiders, you may win converts and new recruits excited to belong where *something is actually happening*. But in such a church, it'll never be quite important enough to invest in the long-term health and discipling of those who belong. For example, if you run a marriage course, it'll really be for evangelism rather than for marriages, so you'll focus more on the 'big picture' of sin (i.e. the fact that we're rebels against God) without addressing the particular sins that might appear in marriage. And more broadly in the church, if there are sins, they'll go unchallenged; if there's conflict, it'll go unresolved. The slow and tedious work of discipling Christians will be left undone, and over time the church will become unhealthy. For a while, it might be a church whose reputation is better than its reality. Eventually, though, you'll realize that if you love your unbelieving friend, the best thing you can do for them is keep them as far away from that church as possible.

The point here is that churches need to be good at both blessing their members and blessing the wider society. Of course, at any given time, a church may be better at one than at the other, but it shouldn't be *bad* at either.

Love is driven by tasks and relationships

In addition, our expressions of love are often shaped primarily either by tasks or by relationships. Where love is driven mainly by *task*, we get to love many people in a few ways. Where it's driven mainly by *relationship*, we get to love a few people in many ways.[13] Let us illustrate.

Many of us do paid work where we get to love many people in a few ways. For example, a plumber may love hundreds or thousands of people a year in the one way of ensuring they have a safe and reliable water flow in their house. An optometrist may supply hundreds of pairs of glasses; a teacher may have dozens of students, and so on.

---

[13] Not all love fits these categories, of course. There's also serendipitous or emergency love, where we love whomever in whatever way we can — fixing a leak in a storm, carrying someone's shopping across a street, or directing a lost child to the information centre in a supermarket. Here the determiner is neither the task nor the relationship, but the circumstance that presents itself. Perhaps the relevant thing here is that this love is less able to be planned (apart from, say, not overplanning your life so as to make such love impossible).

These workers do good to others; their work is a form of love. But it's limited in scope: your plumber, optometrist, or teacher isn't going to come and cook you meals when you fall ill, or help you move house, or give you relationship advice. Of course, all of these jobs involve a level of relationship (because they all involve some degree of human interaction), but the shape of the love is determined primarily by the task: if the plumber I hired last time retires or moves to another town, I can find another who can fix my pipes equally well; when a teacher gets a whole new set of students at the beginning of the school year, in a sense all the relationships have changed, but the tasks of teaching and learning remain largely the same. Because such love requires us to be *competent* at the tasks we're performing, it'll often also be shaped by our giftedness (e.g. Romans 12:3–8).

In contrast, sometimes our love is shaped more by our relationships: for example, the love between husbands and wives, or the love between parents and children (e.g. Colossians 3:18–4:1; Titus 2:1–10). Here, we get to love a few people (e.g. our family members) in many ways. There's no limit to the number of ways nor the extent to which we might be called to love. Of course, these relationships generate many thousands of tasks, but the key driver remains the relationship itself. For example, a parent with a 12-year-old and a 2-year-old will perform very different tasks for each, but all the tasks they perform are determined by the love that a parent has for their children.

Because of our human limitations, we can love only a few

people in these many deep and self-sacrificial ways. Even Jesus only had twelve disciples, and a band of three closer friends within that group. This is another reason to foster friendships in church: outside our families, close friendships are the main kind of relationship where we get to love others in many ways. So if our churches are going to be communities of mutual and sacrificial love, they'll require networks of good-quality friendships.

Love in life, church, and parachurch

As we noted, this book is mostly about love in the local church, but this can't be discussed in isolation. First, individual believers are called to love in all of life (and not just in a local church), and second, the whole people of God are called to love in a range of ways (that go beyond the local church). So when we think about organizing love in church, we have to do so with an eye to these other responsibilities: on the one hand, to the created order (e.g. believers' families, friends, workplaces, nations, etc.); on the other, to those aspects of the Great Commission that eclipse the concerns or the capacity of our local church (e.g. taking the gospel into our workplaces and into all the world).

Love in the various relational networks of our lives

God has given each of us unique circumstances in which to live out our salvation: I alone get to be the husband of my wife and the father of my children; I alone get to be the teacher of this class of students here and now; I alone am called to be a faithful steward of a particular amount of wealth, and so on. But in all these ways that I'm called to love, I'm never really alone: love is always relational (because someone loves someone else), and it's often corporate (because we often work *together* to love others). God has made us in his image to be not just individuals, but individuals-in-community.

So we all belong to a number of relational networks — families, schools, workplaces (including colleagues, clients, suppliers, etc.), neighbourhoods, and nations. As disciples, we need to work out how to be faithful in the various responsibilities that these networks present; this will involve thinking through how the demands of different networks shape one another. For example, if our spouse is depressed or our parents are infirm, this will likely affect the kind and amount of paid work we can faithfully do.

Some of our networks are simply given in the created order (e.g. our biological family); some are determined more by geography (e.g. our local community); some rely more on our giftedness (e.g. our workplace); some are shaped by a combination of factors (e.g. primary schools rely on both demography — i.e. children aged 5–12 and their parents — and geography — i.e. children and parents in a certain locale).

As Christians, we have additional 'new creation' networks: we belong to churches and we participate in parachurch activities. We think different factors influence the shape of our love in these relationships: love in churches is usually determined more by our *identity* as God's people and by our *geography* than it is by our particular gifting or demography; in contrast, love in parachurch often relies more on *gifting* and *demography* than on geography. Let us explain.

Church as a 'Christian neighbourhood'

As we've said, when God saves us, he doesn't just save us as individuals; he saves us into his people. When he includes us in Christ, he also adopts us into his household or family (Ephesians 1:5; 2:6; 1 Peter 2:1–12; Hebrews 12:22–23). We're all integrated into Christ's body, and so we're not just disparate individuals reliant only on him; he's joined us together and we're also reliant on one another (1 Corinthians 12:12–31). This has several concrete implications.

First, the New Testament expects that we belong to a local church — a 'household of God' (1 Timothy 3:5, 15) — where we love our brothers and sisters in many ways. To do this, we have to be close to one another geographically: we're limited in the ways we can love those who live far away.[14] Or to put it another way, if God calls us to love our neighbour, we might think of our local church as a kind of Christian neighbourhood.

Second, our corporate life should express real unity. This is a demonstration of the gospel: the local church is where we can really see whether there's been reconciliation not just between humanity and God, but also between various tribes of humanity. This is a recurrent theme in the New Testament: the gospel overturns the many ways that humans create

---

[14] Of course, there are still *some* possible expressions of love, e.g. we might pray for each other, or share money, or send one another missionaries.

divisions and enmity. We've all been created and redeemed in Christ, and this thoroughly eclipses any differences between us.

So the Apostles explicitly instruct Christians to love one another across the deepest divisions in the ancient world — divisions between Jew and Gentile (e.g. Colossians 3:11; Ephesians 2:14–16), slave and master (e.g. Colossians 3:22–25), and rich and poor (e.g. James 2:1–9). The New Testament contains many instructions to "maintain unity" and to "bear with one another" (e.g. Romans 15:1–3; Ephesians 4:1–6), and it has dire warnings for those who don't (e.g. 1 Corinthians 11:17–30). So we can't be satisfied with speaking fine words about being included in Christ in the heavenlies; we need to show our unity practically in our daily lives. This implies more than just sitting in the same rain shelter at the same time: we actually need to be involved in one another's lives, concretely loving our brothers and sisters in Christ. When we create divisions in our churches — say, according to ethnic background, wealth, education level, or age — we're visibly denying the power of the gospel: we're saying that societal divisions trump our unity in Christ.

Because of our unity and our mutual interdependence, the way I live in my church community is more reliant on my *identity* (as an adopted member of God's household) than on my specific *gifting*. That is, I may be called on to serve in ways that are outside my comfort zone or my area of excellence: I serve according to the needs of my Christian community and of our unbelieving neighbours. For example, I'm not the most gregarious person, but if I'm one of the few people in the church who has a house suitable for hospitality, I'll push myself to be more hospitable than I might otherwise be. Or I'm not very musical, but if there are very few men who can lead our corporate singing, I might put my hand up for that. (Of course, the flipside of this is that my specialized gifts aren't the *primary* factor in deciding whether I should join a particular church. I shouldn't say, "I'm a great musician, but this church doesn't need musicians: I'm going somewhere else.")

All of this suggests a shape for the relationship between individual believers and their churches:

- church can't just be an event to attend; it must also be a community to belong to. A family may hold events (e.g. a Sunday dinner), but you're not *only* a family when you're at the dinner table: your relationships transcend that event. In the same way, church members should see themselves as belonging to a continuous network of loving relationships; they're not just a church when attending an event;
- properly encouraging one another to maturity will take time (i.e. more than a couple of hours a week on a Sunday and on a Tuesday night); it'll take mentoring, modelling, and teaching about the concrete details of life; it'll take the kind of iron-sharpening-iron friendships that we described above;
- part of the role of the Christian community is to equip believers for every aspect of life: that is, part of what it

means for us to spur one another on to love and good deeds is to help one another see how to be godly *outside* church — how to be a loving parent, child, spouse, friend, employee, manager, etc.[15]

Loving the city through parachurch activities

Of course, the local church isn't the only specifically Christian relational network we belong to: many of us are also engaged in parachurch activities. Typically, these are ventures where Christians work together to meet a specialist need that couldn't be met within most local churches — for example, we create theological colleges, welfare agencies, global mission organizations, or evangelistic initiatives within particular industries.

We collaborate for a specific purpose for which God has particularly gifted and equipped us. It follows, then, that while we'd expect our churches to be heterogeneous (brought together uniquely by our union in Christ), we expect that many parachurch networks may look more homogeneous (brought together by our union in Christ *and* by our common gifting or a specific project). Similarly, because church is local, it's primarily concerned with blessing the neighbourhood; because parachurch isn't necessarily local, it might be suitable for some projects which bless the whole city.

This isn't to attach some deep theological significance to cities as opposed to suburbs or towns, and small villages may

[15] This isn't to say that somehow church is *the one* lens through which we view our whole lives, as if 'commitment to Jesus' equalled 'commitment to this Christian community'. This is the sort of theology on which cults are founded.

need parachurch activities, too. Having said this, cities may provide more opportunities (and perhaps a greater need) for such ventures. For example, in smaller towns, it's often possible to invite both non-Christian friends and church friends to a social event. But in the city, this is harder to do: my church is geographically based (i.e. we all live in the same area), but I tend to meet unbelievers through relational networks regardless of geography. For example, I teach ESL in the heart of the city, and my colleagues commute from all over the metropolitan region, so it can be hard to find natural, frequent overlap between my non-Christian friends and my local church.

In such circumstances, I might try to make friends with some other Christians who are in the same relational network, but who belong to other local churches. Together, we could think of ways to promote and proclaim Jesus to our non-Christian friends. For example, I know several other ESL teachers who work in the city, but we all belong to different churches. We've met several times to talk and pray about following Jesus as ESL teachers. This includes discipleship: the particular opportunities to do good and the particular temptations to sin that ESL teachers face. And it includes mission: how together we can bless our colleagues and students. One of us has created an easy-English Bible study in the city. Another has set up a table-tennis room in a pub where city workers and students can get to know one another. And so on.

Of course, geography isn't the only barrier to Christians and non-Christians having overlapping lives. Life-stage can be, too. Take the example of primary schools: it's probably easier to bless a primary school through a parachurch initiative than to try to involve a whole local church. School parents have a common interest and a natural bond: this gives them a good opportunity to build friendships with one another, but it also creates a barrier that excludes people who aren't school parents. So it may be hard to introduce school parents to other members of my church. Meanwhile, if you rounded up all the Christian parents at a given school, they'd probably come from a range of churches.

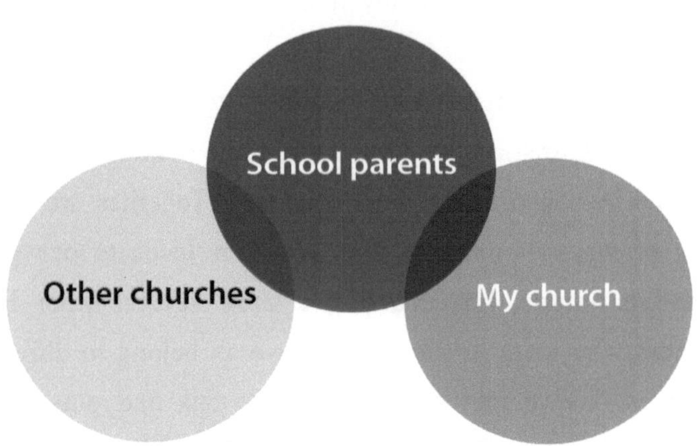

It makes sense in such circumstances to try to get the lives of Christian and non-Christian school parents to overlap regardless of which church the Christians belong to (and with an open-handedness regarding which church any converts might come to belong to). This will require Christian parents from different churches to form friendships, and then to ask how as friends they could bless other families who don't yet know Jesus. Often there are no structures to help us form intentional friendships like these (and in fact, sometimes they're actively discouraged: "You should be spending more time with people in your own church!"). This sort of conflict immediately sharpens the question of how to manage our various responsibilities in church, parachurch, and the rest of life.

Organizing love among individual believers, churches, and parachurch organizations

Many parachurch activities are collaborations between different churches, both at a denominational level (e.g. a theological college, welfare organization, or global mission agency) and at a local level (e.g. churches from different denominations band together to pay for a Scripture teacher in a local high school).

But sometimes church and parachurch can feel like competing priorities: some university students feel torn between the demands of their church and the demands of their campus group; some retirees withdraw from Bible study and Sunday rosters because they're involved in Kairos Prison Ministry. Disputes might arise over where people ought to spend their time, energy, and money, and it's necessary to pray, think, and discuss how best to serve Jesus in the various opportunities he's given us. But it can be tempting to fight over these things because of pride and the desire to build one's own empire, or because of poor communication and disorganization, or simply because of thoughtlessness. With this in mind, here are a few thoughts to help believers harmoniously manage their commitments to both church and parachurch.

Christians are never lone rangers: they're engaged in relationships of mutual care with others in their church. Therefore when they're working out how best to serve Jesus, his people, and his world, they should talk with other believers whom their decisions will affect. For example, if I'm considering embarking on some parachurch venture that's going to take up most of my discretionary time, I need to discuss the implications with my church community.

At the same time, churches don't own believers. (And in particular, leaders don't own the people.) Churches should be open to commissioning members for particular ventures and supporting them (which may include freeing them up from some church responsibilities). This said, those who do paid work for parachurch organizations must also be properly involved in churches. We've known professional missionaries and Bible college lecturers, for example, who've been a bit withdrawn from the life of their church. "My job is my ministry," they say, as if their identity derived not from being included in the body of Christ, but from their specific gifts.

As we weigh up church and parachurch activities, we should be conscious that in church, the main 'unit of mission' is often the family. We expect families to work together to bless those outside the family. We can't ask one member of a family to get involved in any given activity without thinking about the impact this will have on the others. In contrast, in parachurch, the main ‘unit of mission’ is often the individual: I don’t expect my whole family to get involved in my group of Christian ESL teachers, for example.

One of the obstacles to churches partnering in parachurch ventures is that they don’t know about (or are even wary of) one another’s activities. This leads to a lot of duplicated effort. For example, imagine half a dozen evangelical churches whose buildings are within within five to ten minutes’ drive of one another. Each runs its own small youth group, rather than banding together to put on one big one. The same for Christmas carols, and community service (e.g. litter-picking), and training in godliness (e.g. a course on marriage, parenting, or budgeting), and public social events (e.g. showing a film or a sporting event on a big screen). Imagine if they shared their calendars: instead of one good social event a semester, there might be one a month; instead of one training course a year, there might be one a term, and so on. This could provide some more opportunities for relationship-building, for introducing our non-Christian friends to some of our Christian friends, and for Christians to visibly bless the wider society.

This sort of creative and relational thinking about parachurch may open up many more opportunities to bless our neighbours. To develop the primary school example we cited above: with our current church culture, it’s easy to imagine a number of churches getting together to pay for a Scripture teacher. But it’s harder to imagine those same churches helping parents to form inter-church friendships and to cast a vision to promote and proclaim Jesus in that school community. And yet this latter initiative would likely bear a lot of fruit.

A church who love

In this chapter, we've tried to articulate the kinds of love we hope churches are marked by:

- faithful love both in our words and deeds;
- high-quality relationships where we love a few people in many ways;
- good work where we use our gifts to love many people in a few ways;
- love for both the church and the world.

We could map these onto a matrix (with '*words*' in italics). This provides a starting point for assessing where our own church is weaker and stronger.

	Blessing to be in	**Blessing beyond**
Love the few	• Christian family members • a few Christian friends • *conversations*	• non-Christian friends and family • *conversations*
Love the many	• Sunday gatherings • *sermons* • *(many) Bible studies* • youth groups • church-wide parenting course	• *evangelistic courses* • ESL classes • playgroups • being good neighbours (e.g. litter-picking)

Once we've mapped out our church's activities like this, it's also interesting to see how how they intersect with each other, in particular:

1. How words and deeds interrelate;
2. How opportunities to love the many may lead to deeper relationships, and;
3. How the lives of Christians and non-Christians can overlap.

We feel we've already said enough about words and deeds, in our discussions of friendship and of the apostles' witness to Christ through the explained example of their lives.[16] The other two points, however, need to be teased out briefly.

As in Magda's case, it's often possible for a 'love-the-many activity' (e.g. a playgroup) to lead to deeper relationships. This isn't the main criterion for assessing the value of these activities: a playgroup, an ESL class, or a soup kitchen does good, even if it never leads to friendships. But as we serve our neighbours' needs in various ways, we trust that we'll meet a few people who are open to spending more time with us. This is more likely to happen when church members don't just wonder, "How can I get my colleagues to come to the evangelistic event?" but also, "How can I love a few more people in a few more ways?"[17] And of course we'll need to avoid running so many activities that we have no time left for relationships.

---

[16] Though if you'd like more examples, see the Groundwork Everyday course *Leading People to Christ*, especially chapter 2, on the role of the Christian community.

[17] This might change what we think of as 'a win'. Our goal isn't just to get people into the church building or to invite them to an event; rather, it's to take the natural next step of love. So when we assess our church health, we're not just interested in the statistics of how many people came to our events, but of how love and friendship grew.

	Blessing to be in	Blessing beyond
Love the few	• Christian family members • a few Christian friends • *conversations*	• non-Christian friends and family • *conversations*
Love the many	• Sunday gatherings • *sermons* • *(many) Bible studies* • youth groups • church-wide parenting course	• *evangelistic courses* • ESL classes • playgroups • being good neighbours (e.g. litter-picking)

Similarly, Magda's story illustrates some of the effects of allowing our Christian circles to overlap with our non-Christian circles. We're not suggesting here that there's no difference between believers and unbelievers at a theological level. The Bible pictures humanity as divided in two: either you are in Christ, or you are not; either you have the Spirit of God and you own Jesus as your Lord, or you follow the ways of this world and the spirit of disobedience; either you are forgiven, redeemed, adopted, and alive, or you are dead in your sins, cut off from God, enslaved, and stand condemned. But this doesn't mean that our social circles should also be sealed off from one another. We shouldn't hide our 'Christian-ness' from our unbelieving friends; rather, we should seek opportunities for our Christian and non-Christian friends to mix. This will allow our non-Christian friends to witness the love (and the flaws, and the forgiveness) in our Christian community. This could well include talking in 'mixed company' about such things as our work, our money, our friendships, our marriages, our parenting, and our politics. The more these are informed by the gospel, the more of the gospel our unbelieving friends can hear and understand. Magda's friends from the playgroup invited her into their homes and introduced her to other Christian friends socially. In a sense, they'd begun to break down the barrier between 'blessing to be in' and 'blessing beyond'. And it was in this setting of overlapping lives that Magda first really came into contact with Jesus.

<table>
<tr><th></th><th>Blessing to be in</th><th>Blessing beyond</th></tr>
<tr><td>Love the few</td><td colspan="2">• Christian family members
• a few Christian friends
• non-Christian friends and family
• conversations</td></tr>
<tr><td>Love the many</td><td>• Sunday gatherings
• sermons
• (many) Bible studies
• youth groups
• church-wide parenting course</td><td>• evangelistic courses
• ESL classes
• playgroups
• being good neighbours (e.g. litter-picking)</td></tr>
</table>

In the next chapter, we'll explore further why these friendships and overlapping lives don't always 'just happen'. We'll look at why love needs to be organized, and why some of our current structures don't necessarily help.

2. Organizing in church: how social architecture can either promote or impede love

Here's the story of Angela, a member of our church.

She has a number of health problems which affect her ability to carry out physical tasks. One day, her daughter, Lucy, suddenly fell ill and had to go into hospital. Lucy's a single mother, and Angela was the only one available to look after her active two-year-old granddaughter. Another church member got in contact with Angela and asked how we could help. She said that three things in particular would make life more manageable: preparing some meals, cleaning her home, and doing some babysitting to give her a break. A roster was organized and over the next week, about a dozen of us pitched in to perform these tasks.

Structures promote love

Again, there's nothing extraordinary about this story: churches are often good at helping like this in a crisis. But at the same time, it illustrates something of the complexity of loving action. In order for our church to love Angela in this way, we needed three things to come together: desiring to help, knowing what to do, and being organized so we actually did it. We might summarize these as the why, what, and how of love:[18]

- *Why* — why we love. In love, God regenerates us and gives us new hearts — hearts that love him and the things that he loves. So our hope isn't just that we'll do good, but that we'll want to do good. (Without new hearts, we mightn't have done good to Angela. Or perhaps we would have, but grudgingly, or with a view to impressing God or others.)
- *What* — knowing what to do. We need Spirit-transformed minds which can determine what the loving course of action is. (We had to know which tasks in particular Angela needed doing. Without this, we could've expended a lot of effort without actually meeting the most pressing needs; we would've failed to do good to Angela.)
- *How* — how love is facilitated or enabled. We very often need structures or contexts which make it easier — or possible — to love. (Without a roster, it's *extremely* unlikely that so many of us would've 'got around to it'. Or we would've doubled up on tasks on some days and left them undone on others — again, failing to do good.)

So godly action often involves these four elements — the

[18] In this book, we're focused primarily on the *how*, or structures. For more on the heart and mind, see the Groundwork Everyday course *Love and Wisdom.*

action itself; the heart that longs to be godly; the knowledge of what would constitute a godly action, and; the context that enables the action. Picking up the Biblical metaphor of 'walking in Christ' (e.g. Colossians 2:6–7), we might say that the elements are a particular walk itself; the desire to take this walk; the knowledge or ability required to do so, and; various things that enable the walk to happen — a map, street signs, a footpath, suitable shoes, and so on. Of course, there are some walks where no explicit structure is needed, and the same for some godly actions. But there are also walks which are very difficult or impossible without appropriate structures (e.g. orienteering through bushland), and so too for some godly actions.

For example, think about the various ways that I might help people in a developing nation where I don't have any personal contacts. If I want to support the good work of preaching the gospel about Jesus, there are many agencies I could donate to. Similarly, if I wanted to support attempts to reduce poverty in that country, I could give money to a number of non-government organizations. If, however, I wanted to transfer money directly to a poor Christian brother or sister (something suggested in Scripture), I wouldn't know how to proceed. As far as I know, there aren't any organizations that enable this. Here's a good that's either difficult or impossible — not because I don't want to transfer money, nor because I don't know how to make an international payment, but simply because there's no structure to enable it.

Understanding this will help us diagnose why certain

godly actions are rare or absent in our churches.[19] Take the example of intergenerational friendships and mentoring. If our church isn't very good at these:

- it could be a heart issue (I just don't want to disciple younger people);
- it could be a knowledge issue (I really don't know the first thing to do);
- it could be a structural issue (our church is organized such that it's difficult for me to meet and prioritize serving people of different generations. We'll explore this below).

We've noticed that the temptation is to locate most of our failures in the *heart*, with only cursory attention paid to knowledge and structures. Again, all three are necessary, but our main concern in this book is to help reflect on what 'walks' or love don't happen because of structures, and then to suggest some possible solutions.

We're using the word 'structure' in a very broad sense, here. We really mean anything that helps us do a good thing that we want to do and that we know we should do. These include formal structures (such as a church gathering followed by a meal) and informal or cultural structures (such as church members habitually offering hospitality). Further examples are:

- a routine or habit;
- a policy;

---

[19] And perhaps particularly, why our church might do well in a crisis, but less well in various proactive goods — speaking the truth in love, rejoicing and mourning with one another, befriending the socially marginalized, etc.

- a legally incorporated company, with authority, responsibility, and delegation;
- a regular event, such as a Sunday gathering;
- a type of group (such as a Bible study group).

We might overlook the significance of structures because they're less prominent in Scripture than a transformed heart or a renewed mind. But while the Bible doesn't provide a explicit theology of structures, the New Testament does have a number of examples, including:

- widows' lists (Acts 6; 1 Timothy 5);
- putting aside money on the first day of the week (1 Corinthians 16:2);
- if you're sharing a common meal and you're tempted to eat all the food before everyone arrives, eating at home beforehand so you don't exclude people (1 Corinthians 11:34);
- public reading of Scripture, exhortation, and teaching (1 Timothy 4:13);
- church discipline (Matthew 18; 1 Corinthians 5, etc.);
- not being yoked to an unbeliever (2 Corinthians 6).

Some structures — like personal habits — can be imagined and implemented by any individual believer. But where we're looking to co-ordinate love across a whole church, the task of establishing suitable structures really falls to the leaders. Any given church member could take initiative and disciple someone else, but it takes leaders to foster a culture of discipleship.

Leaders promote structures for love

We think that one of the responsibilities of church leaders is to promote love in the churches entrusted to them. And one tool leaders have to this end is the authority to create, maintain, and dismantle various structures.

As leaders think about promoting structures, it's important to see the distinction between *directly bringing about* a certain kind of love and *creating conditions* that encourage love to flourish.[20] Consider our example of delivering meals to Angela. Making a meal is a way of directly doing good; making a roster creates conditions in which many meals can be delivered (even if by itself, a roster produces no food). We might say the same about taxis and taxi ranks. A taxi directly does good by providing a journey; a taxi rank doesn't directly provide any journeys, but it makes it easier or possible for passengers to find a taxi.

Our present church culture seems to favour leaders doing good themselves over creating conditions where the rest of the church can do good. We have an instinct that where we see a need (e.g. discipling women; managing music), we should hire more staff to meet it. For example, we're very likely to pay a children's worker to curate content and design a roster for Sunday school; we're much less likely to invest in training parents to bring up their children in the instruction of the Lord throughout the whole week.

---

[20] We acknowledged Andrew Cameron above for the language of 'creating conditions'; we owe to Mark Baddeley this more specific idea that leadership involves taking responsibility for the conditions under which life can flourish.

If a church's love depends primarily on the staff, it's almost inevitable that it'll also be more focused on events or one-off tasks (i.e. the staff loving many people in a few ways) than on relationships (i.e. where all members love a few others in many ways). At its worst, this can produce an unhealthy dynamic where the staff feel affirmed (because they're desperately needed) and the church feels comfortable (because they've 'outsourced' ministry to the staff). We think a healthier church culture might be focused on:

- not just recruiting volunteers to run church events, but creating conditions where church members are equipped to be disciples and missionaries in their families, friendships, workplaces, schools, sporting clubs, and so on;
- not just welcoming visitors at the door of your Sunday gathering, but creating conditions where church members regularly practise hospitality throughout the week;
- not just doing a one-off marriage enrichment seminar, but creating conditions where church members can talk openly about their marriages, model godliness to one another, and so on;
- not just running a young adults' Bible study, but creating conditions where single people have close relationships of mutual blessing with one another and with families (and where they can have godly courtships, if they wish to pursue marriage);
- not just inviting an unbelieving spouse to a Sunday gathering, but creating conditions where church members love whole families in many ways;

- not just running a youth group, but creating conditions where young people learn from adults of various ages what it means to follow Jesus into adulthood themselves;
- not just visiting an aged-care facility, but creating conditions where elderly and less-mobile people are properly integrated into the life of the Christian community;
- not just putting on an evangelistic event, but creating conditions where there are meaningful friendships between Christians and non-Christians, and where Christians are ready to speak the gospel fluently into the details of their friends' daily lives;
- not just making a donation to the denominational welfare arm, but creating conditions where church members are ready to serve their poor and marginalized neighbours in various ways.[21]

In short, then, we think that churches are likely to grow in love where formal and centralized church activities aren't simply seen as an end in themselves, but as contributing to relationships in which people can love one another. Correspondingly, this requires a shift from thinking about church staff as the main (or only) agents of discipleship and mission, to thinking about how the whole church is engaged in discipleship and mission in their everyday lives. In other

---

[21] We recognize that there are limits to this: our society has professionalized many forms of care, which means that if you don't have professional training, you're constrained in what you can do. Opportunities to serve are limited, but they do exist. Those denominational welfare arms are one place to ask how.

words, organizing love in church is less about about how church members can help the pastor get his work done in the church, and more about how the pastor can help everyone else get their work done in the world.

Before suggesting some structures that we think might help in this regard, we thought it might be worth reflecting on existing social architecture and why it may not necessarily lead to the kind of discipleship and mission we'd like. In our circles, many churches' social architecture relies on two main structures: Sunday congregations and small-group Bible studies. We think that these structures often fail to promote love, and in fact they can even be an *impediment* to love.

The goal of our critique here isn't to suggest that what churches are doing is a complete waste of time, or that God won't bless their initiatives, or that fixing the social architecture will lead to a rosy and problem-free future. We simply want to note that:

- social architecture really does make a difference to our church's capacity to love;
- many of us haven't had the opportunity to intentionally think about or design our social architecture: we've just inherited it from culture or tradition;
- many church leaders may feel a bit frustrated about aspects of their church life: we know how things *ought to be*, and it's not quite how they *actually are*. Changing the social architecture may be part of the solution.

Why Sunday congregations and small-group Bible studies don't always promote love

As we've outlined, fellowship, discipleship, and mission benefit enormously from good-quality friendships. If your church has many such relationships, you don't need to reimagine structures to promote them. But if you lack these friendships, you need to work out why. It could be a heart issue or a mind issue: perhaps people just haven't seen the need for them or don't know how to build them. But it could also be a problem of social architecture: perhaps the existing structures of your church don't promote close relationships.

Consider again intergenerational mentoring. Most of us would say that it's a good thing for older people to invest in and mentor younger people. Yet in many churches, this seldom happens. And the common structures of Sunday congregations plus mid-week Bible studies can make it extremely difficult:

- older and younger often attend Sunday gatherings at different times (i.e. they belong to different 'congregations');
- small groups tend to be made up of people from the same congregation, and so they reinforce the separation of older and younger;
- events designed to bring older and younger together (e.g. a men's breakfast) are infrequent and not designed to provide much opportunity for friendships to grow.

Of course, all this could change and you still mightn't see mentoring: there might simply be an intransigent unwillingness among the older or the younger to invest in each other. It's also possible that mentoring could occur *despite* all this: all it takes is for one person to make the effort to invest in another; regardless of how the church is structured, it's possible for an older person to take the initiative to seek out a younger person, or *vice versa*.

But if they do so and it cuts across the grain of existing structures ("You really should be prioritizing people in your own congregation"), they'll probably struggle to persevere and they'll definitely struggle to recruit others to the same venture. You may end up with a few examples of people being mentored, but you're unlikely to build a whole culture of mentoring.

To broaden this principle out to love in church more generally: wherever you have the word of God and the people of God with the Spirit of God — that is, wherever you have followers of Jesus — you'll have some people sacrificially loving one another. But if you don't build the structures to enable it, you probably won't find a culture of people sacrificially loving one another.

If we want to build a culture that promotes love and godliness, we'll have to think about how our social architecture is either a help or a hindrance. So we need to explore in a little more detail why our Sunday congregations and small-group Bible studies sometimes don't achieve everything we hope they might.

Why Sunday congregations don't always promote love

In our circles, the main organizational unit of many churches is the 'congregation', meaning a group of people who regularly attend a particular Sunday gathering. Notice the overlap of two concepts, here: (1) a particular kind of event (i.e. 1–2 hours with Bible teaching, prayer, sung praise, sacraments, etc.), and (2) a relational network that involves the people who regularly attend that event. We're not so interested here in the style or content of Sunday gatherings; we're interested in how conflating an *event* and *a group of people* can shape the church's social architecture. One obvious implication is that we try to keep congregations small: if they get too big, how could everyone know one another?[22] Our cultural presupposition seems to be that congregations will form communities, and that it'll happen fairly naturally. But it doesn't always turn out that way, and part of the reason may be the design of our Sunday gatherings.

In the critique that follows, it's important to say that we're focused on the nature of the *relational network*, not on *the gathering itself*: whether you place a relatively high value on this gathering (e.g. it's a worship service where you meet God) or a relatively low value (e.g. it's some believers sitting in the same rain shelter to be encouraged to keep following Jesus), we think your gatherings will face similar difficulties from the point-of-view of social architecture: by themselves, they're unlikely to promote high-quality friendships where people love one another in many ways. There are several reasons for this.

---

[22] We may instinctively think that megachurches fail at fellowship, but in fact they don't tie fellowship to their gatherings: that function of church is met through other structures.

First, Sunday gatherings tend to be set up as events to attend rather than as communities to belong to. Therefore church members learn to think of church as something you *go to* once a week rather than something you *belong to* all the time. In most gatherings, we sit in rows looking forward, and we listen to a handful of people talking out the front. We might have a brief chat with a few people afterwards, then say, "See you next Sunday!" There's nothing wrong with this format of gathering *per se* (and in fact it's an efficient way of achieving certain goods), but we must notice that it's not designed to promote deep friendships. Imagine if we tried to foster family relationships this way. It would be very odd if we just got together for a couple of hours once a week, sat quietly and listened to one of the parents give a monologue, then left saying, "Have a good week!"

A second obstacle to congregations becoming communities is the one we've already noted: they're often demarcated along demographic lines. They separate the older from the younger; they divide those with children from those without. This reduces the possibility of intergenerational discipleship, and it makes it very difficult to show the watching world the uniting power of the gospel.

A third challenge for Sunday congregations is that they rely on social conditions that are disappearing. In the past, Sundays were a society-wide day of rest, and so it suited most people to meet that day, and perhaps to eat together or spend the afternoon together. But increasingly, Sunday's becoming 'just another day'. Many of us have to do paid work on

Sundays. Many community-service activities and charity events fall on Sundays. There's a lot of sport on. This cultural shift means that we limit both discipleship and mission if we try to make Sunday gatherings the non-negotiable, defining event of our Christian community. Already, our congregations can be alienating for shift workers, for immobile and ill people, and for new parents. They're not very welcoming for those who have unbelieving spouses (or for the unbelieving spouses themselves). And they don't accommodate non-Christian friends very well: we ask unbelievers to come in to where we feel comfortable at a time that suits us, rather than going out to where they feel comfortable at a time that suits them. So, for example, we've often heard church leaders rail against Sunday sport, saying that if Christians really valued Jesus, they'd 'come to church' instead. But imagine if we thought about sacrificing our preferences for the sake of unbelievers: we may wish to encourage some of our best evangelists to get involved in Sunday sport (and particularly in something like junior lifesaving, which is also a great community service). Of course, this suggestion only makes sense if we separate out 'belonging to a particular Christian community' from 'attending a particular event'.

A fourth reason that congregations often fail to form communities of love is that gatherings tend to be medium-sized — neither small enough to promote loving others in many ways, nor big enough to get a proper economy of scale that facilitates loving many people in a few ways. Again, we're not saying that no one will love anyone else in a congregation:

it's a gathering of people who are transformed by God's love. But notice how a medium-sized gathering (of, say, 100 adults) is too big to love others extensively. With a bit of effort, I can get to know everyone's name and occupation, but I can't get to know much more. I certainly won't have time to learn how to speak the truth in love to all of them, nor will I be able to serve all of them frequently in concrete ways. At the same time, a congregation of this size will be too small to service specialized needs: we're unlikely to have the gifts to provide marriage counselling and addiction recovery and care for people who struggle with mental health issues or who don't have consistent accommodation, and so on. Confronted with the impossibility of everyone loving everyone, we'll likely default to some inadequate habits:

- We might maintain a lot of surface relationships. We're friendly with everyone on a Sunday, but no one really knows what's going on in our lives and we don't really know what's going on in theirs. We never create a culture of loving one another in many ways.
- We might seek to love a few people in a few more ways, but it'll necessarily be a limited number. In this case, many of us will gravitate towards loving those who are easiest to love. There'll be some who valiantly seek to love 'difficult people', but they'll burn out. And some who are difficult to love will simply go unloved.

One solution to this has been to plant new, smaller congregations, and we've belonged to churches who've pursued this strategy. There are two main problems with this, however: (1) Running the entire infrastructure of a Sunday gathering and small groups is exhausting and financially stretching (because new congregations often require more staff). Everyone longs for the church to get bigger so that it'll be more manageable. (2) Even a small Sunday gathering (say, of 50 adults) involves too many people to love properly, particularly in an urban environment where there's a high turnover of church members.

Why small-group Bible studies don't always promote love

It would seem, then, that it's necessary to create smaller relational networks. These might form a kind of 'paddock' that limits the number of people I'm committed to loving in many ways: "All the people in here, love properly." This is often part of the rationale for small-group Bible studies: they make it easier for people to build relationships and care for one another. But again, for several reasons, the design of Bible studies means that they don't necessarily develop into communities where people love one another in many ways.

First, like Sunday gatherings, Bible studies are often designed as an event to attend rather than a community to belong to. Again, our verbs betray us: we *go to* Bible study once a week. (Notice that it would never make sense to say, "I'm going to family.") And when we leave, we say, "See you Sunday!" Moreover, Bible studies are often task-focused: "We're here to study the Bible." This culture can be so strong that we'll pass up relational opportunities in order to be faithful to the task. For example, if there's a major sporting event (like a football final) on the same night as your Bible study, you'll probably feel the pressure to keep going with the study — even though this might be the perfect opportunity for you to spend time with some Christian and some non-Christian friends and watch the game together. And this despite the fact that (between Sunday gatherings and weekly Bible studies) we have about 90 occasions a year where it's easy to study the Bible formally together, but only a handful of occasions where it's easy to get our friendship circles to overlap. If our small groups are designed primarily as events, they may struggle to promote relationships beyond the event.

Second, when we link Bible studies to a particular congregation, it limits their usefulness for relationships. As discussed, they're less likely to be composed of people of different generations. They generally don't include children: they're not something the whole family can belong to. And they're usually considered less important than the Sunday gathering, so we shouldn't be surprised that they don't encourage strong relational commitments between members.

Third, these smaller groups are often made up of 8–12 adults, which can be too many to foster close relationships. It's a good size for a Bible tutorial, but it's too big for most people to have an open discussion about concrete sins or challenges. This is compounded in mixed-gender groups: men in particular seem to be less likely to be honest and vulnerable in front of women.

Finally, Bible study groups tend to have a short life-cycle — often a year. So they don't provide the kind of longevity that good-quality relationships require.

Again, this doesn't mean that *all* Bible studies are a waste of time or that *no one* will love anyone else. Wherever there are people who've been transformed by God's grace, there'll be people who love each other. But these design-flaws in our small groups may explain why we keep thinking, "Bible studies *should* work," even while we reluctantly admit, "But this particular Bible study *doesn't* work very well."

We know that some church leaders in our circles have started to abandon Bible studies because "they don't work". We agree that you shouldn't keep pursuing structures and strategies that don't work. But churches still need to find a way to address one of the real problems that Bible studies are supposed to solve: the problem of creating communities where people express their love for one another in many ways.

If we don't tackle this problem, it's costly for fellowship, discipleship, and mission in general. But we think that the cost is borne disproportionately by certain groups of vulnerable people, including people with disabilities, older single people, single-parent families, 'difficult' people, and those on the fringe.

Our structural failure to care for vulnerable people

This feels like a risky generalization, but in this case we think the risk is worth taking: broadly speaking, the people who are least likely to be well cared for in our prevailing church structures are also the least likely to have a voice in the design of those structures. We'll outline a few particular challenges here;[23] in the next chapter, we'll propose some alternative structures that we think can help address these.

People with disabilities

It can be hard for people with certain disabilities to participate in the life of event-centric churches. For example, if you have difficulty with mobility, just getting to gatherings can be a struggle; on top of this, many church buildings and houses that host Bible studies aren't designed to welcome people with physical disabilities. Similarly, a monologue sermon or an inductive Bible study may not be very accessible to people with an intellectual or a language disability. A person with a social disability, a hearing impairment, or complex communication needs might be overwhelmed by the number of people at a gathering or by the noisy church hall where the morning tea is laid out.

Churches can change various things to make their public meetings more welcoming to people with disabilities, and this is a good start. But it can't be the extent of our love. For some people, the very nature of Sunday gatherings and weekly Bible studies prevents them from participating fully. We'll need to find other ways to promote friendships and mutual edification.

Older single people

In general, younger single people have good opportunities

---

[23] These examples aren't exhaustive — for example, we haven't mentioned those who are marginalized because of ethnicity, socio-economic background or status, religious affiliation, gender, sexuality, etc. The point is, we need to notice our neighbours who are vulnerable in various ways and make the effort to love them properly.

to be relationally connected and make friends in church. They often have more free time than other church members. They may not feel so acutely the tension of living and working in separate locations — on the one hand because they can often live closer to work, and on the other because they have less need to be home by a certain time. This might also make it easier for them to become friends with colleagues outside work time.

In contrast, it's often more difficult for older single people to build good relationships in churches. The way most churches are designed, older single people need to choose to attend Sunday gatherings either with those in the same life-stage (of whom many are younger) or with those of the same age (of whom many are married and have children). Both options pose problems. The difficulty is compounded for Bible studies, where older single people may not even have the option of meeting with married people of the same age: mothers' groups often meet at times that are suitable for children, but not for paid workers. Overall, it means that it's often harder for older single people to form and maintain good-quality relationships in churches, especially with families that include children.[24]

Single-parent families

Single-parent families might also find it difficult to build

---

[24] For more extensive thoughts on some challenges single people face and how churches might help, see either the chapter 'Singleness' in the Groundwork Everyday course *Family*, or http://matthiasmedia.com/briefing/2009/05/making-singleness-better-2/

good friendships. Sunday gatherings can be complicated (especially if there's shared custody of children, and they're only there once a fortnight). Mid-week Bible studies are often impossible. And if a church doesn't have a structured way of helping entire families relate to one other, it's unlikely that it'll 'just happen'.

Families where one spouse isn't Christian

If a church's main way of caring for people is via Sunday gatherings and Bible studies, it may struggle to care for families where one of the spouses doesn't attend formal church events. The believer may feel awkward or ashamed if they have to explain why their spouse isn't there. And there's often no natural social structure that allows the unbelieving spouse to meet other church members outside those formal events (so if they *do* become interested in church things, it can be very intimidating to start coming).

Children

It may seem strange to include children here as a vulnerable group, because many churches put significant resources into teaching and serving them. Paid staff and volunteers provide a range of programmes for young people, and there's often a group of peers and friends. These are good things, and we don't want to downplay them. But churches also have other opportunities to serve children outside formal gatherings, which as a culture we've been less successful at taking up. For example, churches can give training in godly marriage and parenting; they can create conditions where parents are helped in other ways; they can facilitate intergenerational relationships where children are known and loved as whole people (and not just seen as appendages to their parents). Centralized programmes can certainly help children learn about Jesus, but our church will need more than these to thoroughly welcome young people and model for them a life of Christian discipleship.

Difficult people

In God's providence, he's ordained some people simply to be difficult: loving them can be hard work. Of course, God doesn't call us to love *only* difficult people: we hope that many of our friendships will involve mutual service and simple joy. But we must expect that some relationships be more complicated, where the joy is more of the 'joy in suffering' kind. When we meet a difficult person, many of us default to one of two poor responses. Some of us sense the burden of caring for difficult people and we just avoid them. Our lives are full; we know we need to draw the line somewhere, and it's convenient to draw the line just this side of loving a difficult person. On the other hand, some of us feel deeply for difficult people, and so we set about trying to love them all. This is a recipe for burnout. And so overall, the church can end up not caring well for difficult people. (And it often fails to encourage them to use their gifts to love others, too.)

Those on the fringe

Every church has a 'fringe', that is, people who are somehow connected to the church but who for whatever reason don't regularly participate in the church's structures. If our church is primarily organized around Sunday gatherings and weekly Bible studies, it's hard to care well for the fringe, for several reasons. First, we're not sure if they really belong or not: if we measure church membership by Sunday attendance, do we count someone who attends one Sunday in four, or one in six? We may not even be sure if they belong to Jesus: we're tempted to equate 'commitment to Jesus' with 'commitment to these structures', so someone who doesn't turn up every Sunday may look like they're sitting loose to the gospel. And if our church culture expects that we see one another week to week rather than day to day ("See you next Sunday!"), it's almost impossible to love someone who's not around most weeks. If they're followed up at all, it's probably by church staff.

If our existing structures aren't promoting love in the way we'd like, we'll have to imagine some new ones.

Conclusion

We've said here that in order to form loving relationships in church, we often need enabling structures in addition to regenerate hearts and transformed minds. We've outlined some ways that common structures in our circles may fail to promote such relationships, particularly with vulnerable people. In the next chapter, we first outline some 'design principles': what are the salient features of social architecture that we have in mind when seeking to promote love? Based on these principles, we then suggest some structures that may create better conditions for fellowship, discipleship, and mission.

3. Organizing love in church: some concrete suggestions

Before we make some concrete suggestions for improving churches' social architecture, it's worth explicitly laying out our principles and presuppositions. If you disagree with our suggestions, then, this should make it easier to work out why.

Designing alternative structures: making your church simple, small, and large at the same time

The need for simplicity, integration, and co-ordination

Perhaps the most difficult challenge for organizing love in church is the need for *simple, multi-benefit* structures. It's very easy to fall prey to 'feature creep': a church thinks, "We're not doing very well at caring for young people," so they start a youth group. Then they notice that no one's visiting older members of the congregation, so they start a visiting team. And they're struggling to meet unbelievers, so they start a playgroup, and so on. While any one of these structures might be good individually, together they become counter-productive: everyone's so busy keeping the machinery of the rosters running that no one's got time for relationships. It's far preferable to create a few structures that serve multiple purposes, rather than multiple structures each serving a single purpose.

Of course, the structures we have must also be integrated and co-ordinated. It's sometimes possible for a structure to do good in one area, but end up frustrating good in another. For example, take the common structure of a mid-week women's Bible study. In many churches, once women have children, they stop going to Bible study groups at night and start going to a women-only one during the day. In many ways these are good: it's usually easier to take children to something during the day, and it may be easier for women to talk through certain aspects of their lives when there aren't any men there.

But we can imagine circumstances where *even more good* might happen if we didn't run these Bible studies — if instead, women continued to be involved in some kind of small-group structure with their husbands. Assume for a moment that we're able to solve the question of including children in such a group (yes, it's more difficult; no, it's not impossible). And then imagine some good outcomes that become more probable if families stay together:

- It's more likely that women of different life-stages stay involved in each other's lives. This is good because God encourages the younger to learn from the older, and also because people in different life-stages have different gifts (e.g. people without children under five may have more flexible time; single people may have more energy or fewer set demands; older people may be wiser; families may have bigger houses for hospitality, and so on).

- It's more likely that families be able to serve together.
- It's more likely that single women be regularly involved in the life of a family.
- It's more likely that children develop meaningful relationships with adults other than their parents.
- It's more likely that fathers be involved in a small group.

The point here isn't really to comment on women's Bible studies or their value in your church in particular; it's simply that we might end up viewing a particular structure quite differently once we start asking how it relates to everything else we're doing.

The need for small and large relational networks

A second major challenge in designing church structures is working out how to bless both a few people in many ways and many people in a few ways. Smaller groups make it easier to build multi-faceted relationships with a few people; larger groups give us an economy of scale that makes it easier to bless a lot of people through particular projects. So it seems that we need our churches to be both small and big at the same time.

When we say that we need to be small and big at the same time, some of us will be tempted to think first in terms of events: we have small events (Bible studies) and large events (Sunday gatherings). But when we're interested in social architecture, we're really focused on small and large *relational networks*, not small and large *events*. (Of course, networks of any size may host any number of events.)

This means that our structures should be designed in such a way that church members belong to both small and large relational networks at the same time. We might see an analogy again with the family (i.e. I belong both to my nuclear family and to my extended family), or to the workplace (i.e. I belong to a team or division in a larger company or organization).

• • •

In line with these principles, we've made some concrete suggestions of structures that might create favourable conditions for love. We believe these structures can promote love both directly (because they involve people doing good to one another) and indirectly (because they provide the sort of social architecture which can help church members to love God, his people, and his world).[25]

Please note that these are 'suggestions' but also 'concrete': we want to navigate the path between being formulaic and being abstract. If we remained abstract, we wouldn't help anyone actually promote love. (If anything, we'd probably just add to frustration by providing reasons for why love matters.) On the other hand, if we were formulaic, we'd deny that different contexts (in time and place) will require

[25] In this book, we're more narrowly focused on *structures* than on *culture*. However, to help illustrate our ideas, we've included some possible 'habits' that churches could adopt, and here we're straying into cultural renewal. Also, these ideas have largely been worked out iteratively in a series of failed church plants. We haven't successfully implemented all of them ourselves (though we've seen others succeed where we've failed: we suspect we're better architects than builders). And so we'd welcome your feedback: we have no desire to promote fine-sounding theories that have no benefit in real life.

different structures.[26] As we've said, if your church is already good at loving in a particular area, you don't need to create a new structure. But where a church recognizes that they're not doing the good they'd like to — because it's difficult or seems impossible — they probably do need a structure to help it emerge.

No one structure or set of structures is ideal, and every church will need their structures to evolve over time. But we think structures can be 'pretty good' as opposed to 'pretty ordinary'. We've occasionally noticed that when we talk about promoting love in church, some people resist any change on the grounds that "there's no perfect church or church model." It's true that nothing's *perfect*. But we do think there's such a thing as *good enough*. Consider governments and nations, for example. None of them is perfect, and yet some countries are much better to live in than others. We're proposing that churches pursue structures that are good enough in their particular time and place, rather than settling for a *status quo* that doesn't adequately help us follow Jesus.

In light of chapters 1 and 2, we think that 'good enough' church structures create conditions where:

- we get to love a few people in many ways (both as a blessing to be in and a blessing beyond);
- it's possible to pursue friendships, meaningful conversations, overlapping lives, blessing, and focused learning;

---

[26] Not least, we're conscious of different difficulties faced in the city and the country. If you live in a rural area where there's a relatively low population and residents live in the same place for decades, you face different challenges from an urban context where there are more people than you could reasonably recognize (let alone meet or befriend), and people constantly move in and out.

- a heterogeneous group of people can concretely display their unity in Christ;
- vulnerable people are less likely to fall through the cracks — in fact, they're encouraged and enabled to love Jesus, his people, and his world.

Gospel communities: for everyday fellowship, discipleship, and mission

Our first suggestion is that local churches create within them a number of smaller communities.[27] The aim is for these to function in a very church-like way: that is, as heterogeneous groups of people who commit together to discipleship, fellowship, and mission. Although we're not completely happy with the term, for the sake of brevity we'll call these 'gospel communities'. In the following paragraphs, we'll sketch what a gospel community might be like, along with how we think it can promote love.

It's important to note at the outset that we expect gospel communities to take time — perhaps years — to form properly. They'll require a change in the culture of the church, so that people identify as a community of disciple-making disciples. There'll need to be explicit and consistent teaching and modelling along these lines. Knowing that the intended shape or 'end goal' of these groups will take time to emerge, we've suggested a few steps to take along the way: the first few things you could introduce to an existing Bible study group,

---

[27] Here we're just using the term 'local church' to describe what actually exists at the moment; we're not seeking to justify or critique this on theological grounds.

say, to begin to encourage one another further in Christian faithfulness and maturity. If we're going to make concrete suggestions, we want them to be practicable.

A community that's open (including to children)

The kind of gospel communities we're suggesting are open and inclusive: in principle, anyone could join them. As we've discussed, the good news about Jesus binds together people who are unlike each other. And as much as possible, a gospel community reflects and expresses our common identity as followers of Jesus.

This doesn't mean that a group needs to be artificially manufactured to have the greatest possible diversity: even if this were possible, it's likely the group would end up too big. Moreover, in cities, many suburbs tend to be *somewhat* homogeneous (e.g. a majority of people share an ethnicity or a socio-economic background), and we would expect the church to reflect the flavour of the surrounding suburb. But there's a difference between a gospel community that has a certain flavour (by accident) and a group that's exclusive or targeted (by design). For example, there's a difference between a group that includes quite a few young, single professionals and a group that is *for* young, single professionals.[28]

In this mix, we expect gospel communities to include families, and therefore children. This doesn't mean that every

---

[28] As we outlined in chapter 2, however, we think there may be good reasons to undertake some evangelistic ventures in more homogeneous groups (e.g. workplaces or industries), simply because this follows the relational contours of a city. But these ventures aren't churches or gospel communities.

activity of a group needs to include children, or that there aren't good reasons to have events just for adults or just for children. But it does mean that at some profound level, when you think of who is in your group and who you belong to, you include the children. This inclusion should be reflected and expressed in real ways, such as: having conversations with children, finding out about their world, their desires and their fears; practising with them as they learn to ride a bike, hit a ball, or paint a scene; including them in conversations about Jesus; praying with them and for them; singing songs they know and like.

A community that's a relational network rather than a series of events

A gospel community isn't formed by *attending an event*, but by *belonging to a network of relationships*: it's an identifiable group of people who've committed to love one another and to love others together. So you can belong to a gospel community even if you can't always attend a Sunday gathering (e.g. shift-workers; less mobile people). And members of gospel communities might attend different Sunday gatherings.[29] (In fact, we might even design the groups in just this way, because Sunday gatherings often tend towards homogeneity, due to the

---

[29] We realize that this is an eccentric idea in our circles. We understand (but so far aren't convinced by) the argument that there's something constitutive about the Sunday gathering and hence it's still a 'congregation'. If that's your theological conviction, we still think you'll need smaller relational networks as well — i.e. gospel communities — but you'll want to make sure that gospel community members also attend the same Sunday gathering (and presumably find ways to discourage homogeneity both in the gatherings and in gospel communities).

timeslot, the format, the music, the 'vibe'.)

Because it's a relational network, a gospel community exists continuously (rather than, say, running on an annual cycle, as many Bible studies do). Depending on the needs and limitations of the members and of their non-Christian friends, different gospel communities may have different scheduled activities — e.g. a lunch or dinner with Bible teaching once a week, once a fortnight, or once a month, where most people would be expected to come if they could; a weekly prayer breakfast where we know only a few can come; an open home on Thursday evenings where we look to invite unbelieving friends, etc. It might also be good to have some common tasks to share in (e.g. a lot of us volunteer at the same op-shop; we help teach ESL to local migrants), because one of the key ways we build friendships with one another is by serving together over time. But these activities don't define the group: we wouldn't expect everyone to be at every scheduled event. And whatever regular events we do have, we would expect there to be lots of space for people to initiate their own *ad hoc* interactions with a few other members of the gospel community.

A community that gathers

Having said all this, we still expect that gospel communities will need to gather regularly for formal Bible teaching, prayer, maybe singing, possibly a meal (including, perhaps, meals during which we remember Jesus' death with bread and wine). This is part of how we express our identity as people who belong to Jesus and to each other; it's one means of encouraging one another in Christ. We think such formal gatherings should be *regular*, but this doesn't necessarily mean *weekly*. In fact, if your church has a weekly Sunday gathering, we think there may be benefits to gospel communities gathering less frequently.

If you live in a place where people's lives are complicated and busy, then adding formal weekly events will probably come at the expense of more informal relational time. This is difficult to communicate, because we can easily imagine losing a good thing we already have (i.e. "I really like my weekly Bible study. It wouldn't be nearly as good if it were fortnightly"), but it's harder for us to imagine a good thing we've never had (i.e. "What would the benefit be if I could invite some neighbours over for a meal?"). But good relationships require informal time — an unexpected chat with a child on the walk home from school; banter between fans of rival sporting teams; discovering a shared delight as you browse through a friend's bookshelf.

A second reason not to gather weekly is to make it easier to meet the needs of children and parents. Including children and adults in the same event presents difficulties; trying to do so every week may make those difficulties seem insurmountable.

A community that's coherent, identifiable, and smallish

If we're going to commit to loving a few people in many ways, we need to identify who those 'few people' are, and a gospel community helps us create a suitable boundary. This isn't *exclusive* (that is, it's not a cult; we still have friends and others outside the gospel community whom we love sacrificially), but it is *suggestive* (that is, if I'm wondering what to do this weekend, I might say "no" to catching up with some of the 200 Christian Facebook friends I have from previous churches, and "yes" to sharing a meal with some people from my gospel community and a non-Christian friend). So we don't love *only* the members of our gospel community, but we do love *at least* them.

But 'few' is a vague term. As a rule of thumb, we think gospel communities:

- should be small enough that it's possible to love everyone in the group. That is, small enough to promote good-quality relationships where we can love one another in many ways, being a blessing to be in and a blessing beyond. But at the same time, they;
- should be large enough to feel like a community, rather than a small university tutorial. There should be a range of possible relationships (i.e. I'm likely to find a friend), a sense of relational stability (i.e. it doesn't feel like this group is going to fall over at any moment), and a mix of gifts.

So if there's a 'magic number' for the size of a gospel community, it's a number that will change from context to context. It depends on how transient people are, how large their houses or other available meeting places are, how busy they are, and how many responsibilities and relationships they typically have outside church.

We suspect that for most churches in cities, the magic number will be somewhere between 15 and 40 people (including children). Some questions that might help you assess the size of the group are:

- If someone needs help, do I think, "I am part of the solution"? (If I think, "Someone else (probably the church staff) will take care of it," then the group may be too large.)
- Do I have the opportunity to serve some community members in more ways? (If I'm looking to reduce or 'manage' the number of people I love, then the group may be too large.)
- Do we get to see one another often and know one another well enough that we can speak the truth in love to one another? Can we encourage one another to follow Jesus in concrete ways (e.g. give detailed advice on career, money, marriage, and parenting) and call one another to repent of specific sins? (If I feel like I'm having a lot of fairly shallow social interactions, then the group may be too large.)
- Have we got time and energy to get to know and bless one another's unbelieving friends in many ways? (If all our efforts are spent serving the needs of the group, and not on being a blessing beyond, then the group may be too large.)[30]

---

[30] Of course, there may be other reasons that the group is unhealthy — to do with the heart or mind, or even just the incompatibility of personalities.

Having noted some problems of being too large, it's important to reiterate that we think it's possible to be too small. Groups that are too small may be either too intense (because we spend too much time together) or too disparate (because there weren't enough people for everyone to find a friend fairly quickly). In addition, we noted that gospel communities need a mix of gifts, and that demands a certain number of people. In particular, we think some gifts are disproportionately important in a gospel community (to the point where their absence may be fatal to the group), namely:

- evangelism — you need people who find it relatively easy to form friendships with unbelievers and easy to share the gospel. Without these, groups may become insular and ineffective in mission;
- hospitality — you need people who find it relatively easy to create a kind of social hub. Perhaps they're good at making meals; perhaps they live somewhere where it's easy to invite others. When community members experience the benefits of hospitality, it's easier for them to make the effort to be hospitable themselves (and they have a model to follow). But if no one in the group is gifted this way, it's hard to get the culture started.

A community that loves (including vulnerable people)

A gospel community is designed to create conditions for fellowship and discipleship: we commit to loving one another in word and deed. We share life: we expect to have meals together throughout the week, to read God's word and to speak the truth in love to one another, to pray together, to socialize together, to meet practical needs (e.g. to do shopping for less mobile members; to babysit; to help move house, etc.).

It's also a group who commit to loving outsiders together. We expect to get to know and serve one another's non-Christian friends and family, too. This helps us move away from the common mission strategy of attempting to reach 'people groups' (e.g. 'leaflet the suburb', 'adopt a block', 'evangelize postmoderns', etc.). This strategy almost inevitably implies a 'build it and they will come' mentality: we put on an event that we think will appeal to a certain type of person, and we hope that some actual people turn up. In contrast, a gospel community gets to show and tell Christ's love to actual people — our friends (who may have some things in common with various people groups, but who are never mere stereotypes). In addition, we're likely to see more and better evangelism if we use our gifts together to be a blessing beyond ourselves. Some of us are more gifted evangelists than others. And some are better than others at creating conditions in which evangelism can take place — some of us are better at hospitality, some of us have houses where meals can happen, some of us are good at organizing social events, some of us are good at spending time with social outcasts, and so on. As we work together, we'll create relationships and opportunities for evangelists to speak.

And a community of love like this can develop excellent conditions in which to care for vulnerable people. To revisit briefly the groups we explored in chapter 2:

- We said some people with disabilities might be excluded in various ways from 'one size fits all' church events. The relational network of a gospel community is much more likely to allow them to serve and be served according to their particular gifts and needs. For example, if someone in a gospel community has mobility difficulties, meeting times and places — whether for formal or social gatherings — can be arranged to suit them. People with intellectual or language disabilities can hear God's word taught in ways that they learn best. And significantly, they can also have the time and relational capital that allows them to speak God's word to others. Similarly, people with social anxiety or complex communication needs can build deeper friendships with a few people over time, rather than struggling to contribute to small talk with a different crowd week by week. And so on.
- Older single people will have a stable network of others — including elders, peers, and children — to provide a family-like set of relationships.
- Single-parent families could be blessed by people in different life-stages who are actively looking to serve them. Not least, there are likely to be other parents who can be sounding boards or role-models in the difficult task of raising children.
- Unbelieving spouses would have a ready context in which to become friends with other Christians and to be shown the love of Christ in many ways.

- Difficult people can be loved well by other members of the gospel community. The group is small enough that I won't be tempted to ignore them (because if someone has a problem, I feel like I'm part of the solution). But at the same time, the task of caring for them falls to 20 people rather than two or three, so no one feels overwhelmed. In addition, a gospel community provides opportunities for difficult people to use their gifts to serve others.
- Gospel communities massively increase the church's capacity to care for those on the fringe. If our gospel community knows that it's responsible to look out for some particular fringe-dwellers, it can organize itself to do so. 20 adults could easily care for four people on the fringe, whereas a congregation of 200 would never be able to care for 40.

A community that grows in godly habits

For some of us, it will seem like an impossible leap to go from our current Bible studies to gospel communities. One way to stage a change is to imagine some habits that might begin to reshape the culture of the group. Depending on how quickly habits were adopted, you might be able to introduce a new one every three to six months. Consider these four habits, for example, which could be introduced over one or two years:

1. At least once a month, everyone in this community will aim to see at least one other member outside the formal meeting time (e.g. have a meal together; go to a film).

- This helps to build friendships.

- It develops the sense that this group isn't just something I *go* to; it's something I *belong* to.
- It begins to provide a context for godly modelling (e.g. if I come to your house, I might see you dealing respectfully with your spouse or graciously with your children).

2. At least once a month, everyone in this community will aim to have at least one meaningful interaction with at least one Christian and one non-Christian together (e.g. invite a non-Christian friend to come to a meal with others from my gospel community; invite a Christian friend to join me and my work colleagues at pub trivia).

- This helps build friendships with unbelievers.
- It allows unbelievers to witness the love between believers ("By this everyone will know that you are my disciples..."; John 13:34-35).
- It changes how you talk and pray together about mission (because now I know your non-Christian friend, and maybe they're my friend, now, too).

3. At least once a month, everyone in this community will try to speak the truth in love to someone else (i.e. encouraging, correcting, rebuking, training in righteousness in the details of someone's real life; having a meaningful conversation about some aspect of life under Jesus — work, money, marriage, parenting, sexuality, conflict, friendship, political engagement, church, etc.).

- This is at the heart of how discipleship and mission happen. It's not just an abstract presentation of the gospel in metaphysical terms (i.e. a gospel tract); it's learning how Jesus speaks a word of hope, or joy, or judgment, or comfort *to you in your circumstances*. It's where you get to talk in a meaningful way about what it means to love Jesus and follow him in the everyday. (This is equally applicable to believers and unbelievers.)

- This is almost impossible to do if the first two habits aren't in place: I don't know how to encourage you or rebuke you very well if I don't know you very well. And it's easier for you to hear my words as loving if they come in the context of a loving relationship.

4. At least once a month, everyone in this community will look for one opportunity to serve someone sacrificially (e.g. make some meals, do some gardening or painting, help to move house, visit a shut-in or a 'difficult person', give a lift to the airport, pay a bill, do some babysitting, etc.).

- The person I serve might be a member of the community or someone beyond.
- This gives the perfect opportunity for several members of the group to work together to bless someone else (e.g. by gardening together). This in turn helps to build relationships.
- It could be a regular commitment (e.g. three of us are going to serve together once a month at a soup kitchen and try to get to know some diners and some other volunteers, or; we're going to do a weekly ESL conversation class together, and look and pray for one or two ESL learners and teachers whom we can befriend outside the class).

A community where most of our church fellowship, discipleship, and mission happens

In brief, then, a gospel community is a structure that facilitates the bulk of the ordinary Christian life: it creates conditions that help Jesus' followers to love one another and to love outsiders together. Because it fulfils most of the functions of church, we might think of it in a way as 'the most church part of church'.[31]

We noted in the previous chapter that many churches have as their basic unit of social architecture the Sunday congregation; derived from this are smaller Bible study groups. If you asked the question, "Who's part of this church?", the answer would be, "The people who come to Sunday gatherings (a certain percentage of the time)."

We're proposing an inversion of this, where a smaller relational network — the gospel community — is the basic unit of social architecture. On this model, when you ask, "Who's part of this church?", the answer is, "Those who belong to a gospel community (all the time)." This has implications for how you communicate the membership of the church. The Sunday-centric church might say, "About 80% of our church are in small groups"; a church composed of gospel

[31] At this point, we've drifted away from a discussion purely of social architecture and into the territory of ecclesiology. We don't have space here to properly address important questions about the definition or *form* of church. If you disagree with the language or idea of a gospel community being 'the most church part of church' (e.g. because you define the local church by a certain kind of word ministry, or worship, or polity), we hope that you agree with us about the kinds of fellowship, discipleship, and mission that should be present in your church community. So if the defining aspect of your church (e.g. a Sunday gathering) doesn't achieve all these ends, other aspects of your church life will seek to do so. (This means that it's possible to reject the idea that a gospel community is the most church part of church, but still make it the basic unit of social architecture.)

communities will say, "Our Sunday gatherings attract about 125% of our church membership."

If you agreed with us on this, it might also have implications for how you thought about pastoral oversight. In a church made up of gospel communities, the line of pastoral responsibility and authority isn't drawn faintly around those who turn up to a certain percentage of Sunday gatherings, but starkly around those who are members of the community (regardless of how many gatherings they can attend). This sort of pastoral oversight requires gospel communities to be *led* rather than merely *facilitated*. Ideally, they should be led by men who meet the Biblical qualifications for eldership (but who might never meet the contemporary standards for being paid pastors, e.g. no formal theological training; no ability to run a non-profit organization with 100 volunteers, various properties, and so on). Leaders may have a couple of trainees or apprentices, too, so that succession and scaleability are built in.

Of course, we recognize that to begin with, this sort of eldership may not be available: churches will have to deal with the real circumstances they're in. It might mean, for example, that one elder or a paid pastor lends oversight to several groups for a time. In such a setting, though, equipping new elders would be a matter of urgent prayer and focused training.[32]

[32] We should remember the context in which the Biblical standards for eldership are delivered (Titus 1; 1 Timothy 3; cf. 1 Peter 5; Acts 14:21–23). The men appointed elders in some churches may have been converted only weeks or months earlier, but presumably knew how to teach and how to manage their households well (e.g. as good husbands, fathers, masters, stewards, etc.). We need to assess people not so much by government-accredited awards (e.g. a Bachelor of Theology), but by the suitability of their character and gifts for the task at hand (here, leading a gospel community).

• • •

If we return to the elements of the process of love that we outlined in chapter 1, we can begin to map out how these proposed structures help to promote love. (We've also included parachurch ventures to show that the local church isn't the only context for Christian discipleship and mission.)

	Friendships	Overlap-ping lives	Blessing	Conversations	Learning
Mission	• GC • Ventures • (All of life)	• GC • Ventures	• GC • Ventures	• GC • Ventures	• GC
Discipleship	• GC (partly) • Ventures	• GC • Ventures	• GC • Ventures	• GC (partly)	• GC • Ventures

We're conscious that we haven't included Sunday gatherings, yet; we'll return to those soon. Meanwhile, note that we've said that a gospel community might only *partly* promote friendships and meaningful conversations. This is because if a gospel community includes up to 40 people, it may be too big to quickly create close friendships — the kind of iron-sharpening-iron and intergenerational friendships we touted in chapter 1. Consequently, it might not always be the best context for meaningful conversations about all the details of our lives (and especially not at first, when relationships and culture are forming). The formal gatherings of a gospel community are unlikely to facilitate discussion of more sensitive issues of godliness: like Bible studies, they're too big, and they include men, women, and children. In such a group, it's almost impossible to have the level of trust required for vulnerability and admission of sins. We therefore think it's worth having a second structure specifically to promote friendships, conversations, and learning for the purposes of discipleship.[33]

A discipleship group: for friendship, conversation, and focused learning

Again, we've struggled to find a good name for this structure, but the basic outline is simple enough:

- Every month
- 3–5 people of the same gender come together
- to discuss an article, book chapter, talk, or video on some aspect of life;[34]
- to pray;
- and to each identify one concrete area of life where they can grow in love or godliness over the next month. This might be a habit (e.g. healthier eating with the children; not speaking harshly to my spouse; praying daily…). It might be a specific project (e.g. "I need to reconcile with my sister"; "I'm going to set up my bank accounts and

[33] It's perhaps worth noting that this isn't merely a theoretical observation: in practice, when we've tried to form gospel communities, we've found that this sort of relationship and conversation often hasn't just happened organically: it's required an additional structure.

[34] We think this is preferable to an exegetical Bible study because (a) we're assuming that people are learning the content of Scripture elsewhere (e.g. in expository teaching on Sundays, and in personal or family devotions), and (b) we think that learning godliness in the various spheres of life usually requires reflection on the *whole* witness of the Bible, rather than just one passage.

budget properly so that I can be more generous"). Other members of the group can provide advice, support, encouragement, and 'accountability'. And it may be good if, say, once or twice a year, the whole group works on a similar area of love (e.g. hospitality) or on the same project.

- At least one other time in the month, each person also seeks to do something social or life-sharing with at least one other person in the group.

From the point-of-view of a church member, this structure might be beneficial in several ways:

- It creates conditions that promote high-quality relationships and significant conversations.
- It helps you do some ethical reflection as you work through useful, integrated content.
- It provides the movement from reflection to application and action, which might help you make actual changes.
- It encourages you to focus on one area of godliness or develop one new habit at a time.
- One person could be involved in several groups, and so build relationships with people from church, people from a parachurch network, or maybe even a non-Christian friend who'd find it easier at first to engage with an applied topic (e.g. "Are you interested in what we might learn about parenting from Jesus?") than with an exegetical Bible study (e.g. "Would you like to join our Bible study on 2 Corinthians for four weeks?").

From the point-of-view of a leader who's thinking about the social architecture of the whole church, this structure has additional advantages:

- It can promote relationships that are otherwise quite difficult: groups can be intergenerational; they can be 'cross-cultural' in different ways (e.g. across ethnic or socio-economic divides); they can include Christians from different churches; they're flexible and welcoming to the various groups of vulnerable people we mentioned in chapter 2.
- It's easy to adopt. Anyone should have the time and competence to be involved in one of these groups. People who feel they can't commit to a weekly Bible study could still make time once a month. Because of the small size of the groups, if a number of people can't make it, it's possible to reschedule rather than simply miss it. This may make it easier for people with irregular life commitments.
- It's replicable: groups can multiply quite easily as they get bigger, and (perhaps more importantly) some people can be in two groups at once. This means they could start the multiplication process while being able to stay in a group for a longer period of time.
- The structure's simple to understand and communicate.
- It's cheap or free.
- It has a low bar for leadership. A group needs *some* leadership (i.e. someone to select content; someone to co-ordinate meeting time and place), but it's a long way short

of the requirements for Biblical eldership, and so a lot of people would be qualified to run one.

- Some church leaders could be involved in *many* groups, which would help them develop meaningful relationships with a lot of people in their church.

It should be clear from some of the examples we've cited that we don't think this structure needs to be tied to gospel communities: you could meet with people in other gospel communities, other churches, parachurch ventures, and so on. So, adding discipleship groups (DG) to our table:

	Friendships	Overlap-ping lives	Blessing	Conversations	Learning
Mission	• GC • Ventures • (All of life)	• GC • Ventures	• GC • Ventures	• GC • Ventures	• GC
Discipleship	• GC (partly) • Ventures • DG	• GC • Ventures • DG	• GC • Ventures	• GC (partly) • DG	• GC • Ventures • DG

These two structures — gospel communities and discipleship groups — are designed to promote small relational networks and loving a few people in many ways. We turn now to consider how a larger relational network across a whole local church might also be used to bless many people in a few ways.

The local church as a basecamp

If a church wanted to adopt something like our framework

for gospel communities, they'd probably need more than one: most churches have more than 15–40 people in them. And we think that it makes sense to have a number of gospel communities networked together into a single church — that is, for church members to see themselves belonging at the same time to a smaller relational network (a gospel community) and to a larger one (say, St Agatha's Church).

A larger relational network allows economy of scale: we can share various resources (e.g. buildings, staff, bank accounts, administration overheads); gospel community leaders can share in the oversight of the whole church; we can pool our gifts, which may help us be more diverse in the kind of love-the-many activities we can undertake.

The most obvious example of a love-the-many activity is a public gathering (typically weekly, on Sundays), where we share our gifts and worship God as we hear his word, praise him in song, pray, baptize, and so on. But other activities beyond these Sunday gatherings are possible, too.[35] We may do various kinds of specialist training, e.g. the network might run seminars on marriage, budgeting, or Biblical counselling. There's an obvious need for leadership training and support: compared to congregations, gospel communities require more leaders, though they probably require fewer staff. This training and support could fall to the whole network, rather than to any

[35] At the same time, it probably makes sense to maintain *very few* of these activities, so that the organization as a whole has the capacity to do everything well, and so that individuals have the capacity to properly commit to and work with gospel communities.

one gospel community. And as a network grows, we may find more outside-the-box opportunities. For example, a church might develop a business co-operative — a group that encourages relationships so that business people across the network can benefit from one another's experience. It might even pool some start-up capital and create some new businesses to bless the wider community. (Of course, this could also work as a parachurch venture, involving Christians from other churches, and perhaps the non-Christian community, too.)

A larger relational network also allows for love-the-many activities that bless those outside the church. For example, we might do such things as put on open-air cinema nights, build a website for local retailers, get involved in local government, run a boarding house, an op-shop, or an after-school care. (Again, we might look to partner with nearby churches and other organizations on some projects.)

In this way, the larger relational network of the local church — and particularly the centralized apparatus of staff, real estate, etc. — could be viewed as a kind of basecamp (BC). Its primary role isn't to do all the discipleship and mission itself; it's to equip and resource the members of the local church to love in various ways. This includes running love-the-many activities and church-centred activities (e.g. Sundays). But it also means creating conditions that help church members develop love-the-few relationships and to follow Jesus in their everyday lives.

	Friendships	Overlap-ping lives	Blessing	Conversations	Learning
Mission	• GC • Ventures • (All of life)	• GC • Ventures	• GC • Ventures	• GC • Ventures	• GC • BC: Sundays • BC: Specialist structure (e.g. evangelistic course)
Discipleship	• GC (partly) • Ventures • DG	• GC • Ventures • DG	• GC • Ventures	• GC (partly) • DG	• GC • Ventures • DG • BC: Sundays • BC: Specialist structure (e.g. parenting course)

As an aside, a network of gospel communities is also far easier to scale than a congregation-based church. That is, most congregations tend towards being medium-sized: they seem to have an upper limit of around 200 (depending on the gifts of the staff and the demographics of the members). If they get any bigger than this, the pastor can't even remember everyone's name, let alone pastor them, and congregation members have trouble knowing who's a member and who's a visitor. But there's not the same theoretical limit on the number of people who could belong to a network of gospel communities, nor the same costs to multiplying:

- If everyone belongs to a gospel community, there's less pressure on the Sunday gathering to provide fellowship. So when the building starts filling up, it's much less costly to start an additional gathering in another timeslot. (This would lead to a much more efficient use of buildings, as well as of the time and effort of staff and volunteers);

- When you need to create a new gospel community, you can probably 'shave' members from several other gospel communities, rather than splitting one community in two (or tossing all of them up in the air and starting again). This allows for continuity of relationships.

A visual summary of the proposed structures

In the preceding section, we showed how our suggested structures map onto the elements of love from chapter 1. We think it's also worth showing how these structures help God's people to lead coherent, faithful lives in his world. To this end, we've created a diagram in two parts.

In the first part, we've mapped out several aspects of the ordinary Christian life.

- At the centre is Jesus: all of life revolves around him and is lived under him, to his glory.
- The innermost ring (FOLLOWING JESUS) represents the life of an individual disciple — living out our salvation with our responsibilities as a friend, child, spouse, parent, worker, neighbour, citizen, etc. At this point, the diagram is divided to indicate those forms of love which are directed more towards LOCAL COMMUNITIES (i.e. our geographical neighbours, in the lower half) and more towards the WIDER CITY (the upper half).

- The middle ring (FOLLOWING JESUS TOGETHER) represents the various ways that disciples co-operate to love Jesus, his people, and his world.
- The outermost ring (FOLLOWING JESUS TOGETHER IN THE WORLD) reminds us that the people of God are still *human*: we live in the world and are called to bless the world.

Of course, the boundaries between these various aspects of life are fuzzy and porous: no actual life can be neatly segmented in this way.

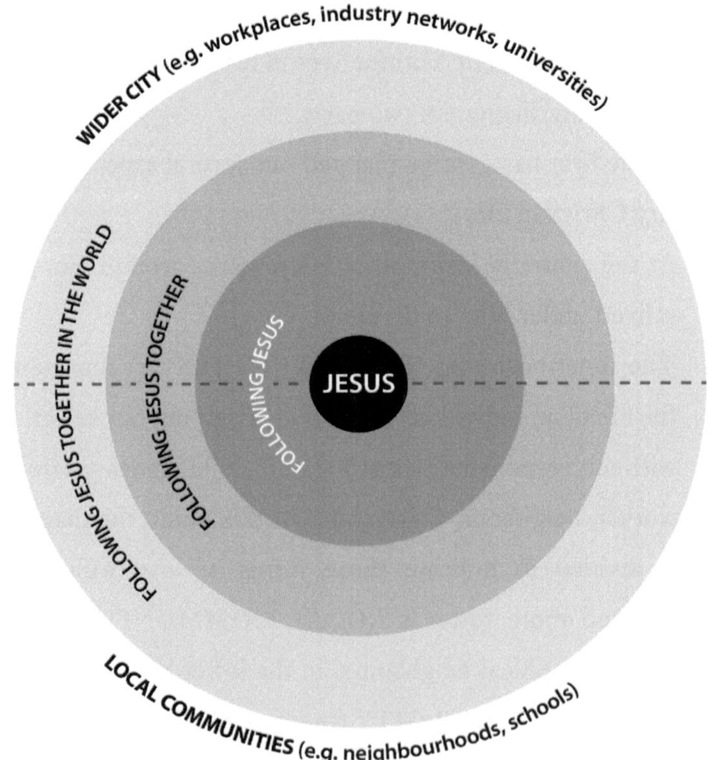

In the second part of the diagram, we've populated each ring with some paradigm examples. We've also included the various structures outlined in this book, showing how they promote love in different ways and different areas of life. (We should be explicit that these are descriptions of what typically happens, not prescriptions of what we think *should* happen.)

- Family is a paradigm example of loving a few people in many ways. Families are also *local*: they're the basic unit of mission in the local church, and they belong to gospel communities together. Families also love the wider community independent of the church (e.g. they belong to schools; they frequent local businesses, etc.)
- Friendships are another paradigm example of loving a few people in many ways. Friendships, however, aren't necessarily bound by geography in the way that families are. As well as being in themselves a good gift to all humanity, friendships can promote personal godliness and provide opportunities for mission; they're collaborative, and; they can create conditions to bless both neighbours and the whole city.
- Work is the paradigm example of loving many people in a few ways. Some people's work is local (e.g. I work in a shop near where I live), but many workplaces allow love in the wider world.
- Gospel communities and churches are primarily designed to promote *local* discipleship and mission — as they equip individual believers for godliness in all of life; as church members love one another; as together church members love their unbelieving neighbours.

- Parachurch ventures, however, can promote love in the city. They're dependent not so much on *geography*, but on *demography* and *gifting* (e.g. Christians in the same industry banding together to promote and proclaim Jesus). Of course, some parachurch ventures are local (e.g. Christian school parents from several churches banding together to bless their school community).
- Discipleship groups are primarily designed to promote individual godliness, but they might be composed of people whose relationship is local (e.g. Christians who live in the same suburb) or city-wide (e.g. Christians who work in the same industry).

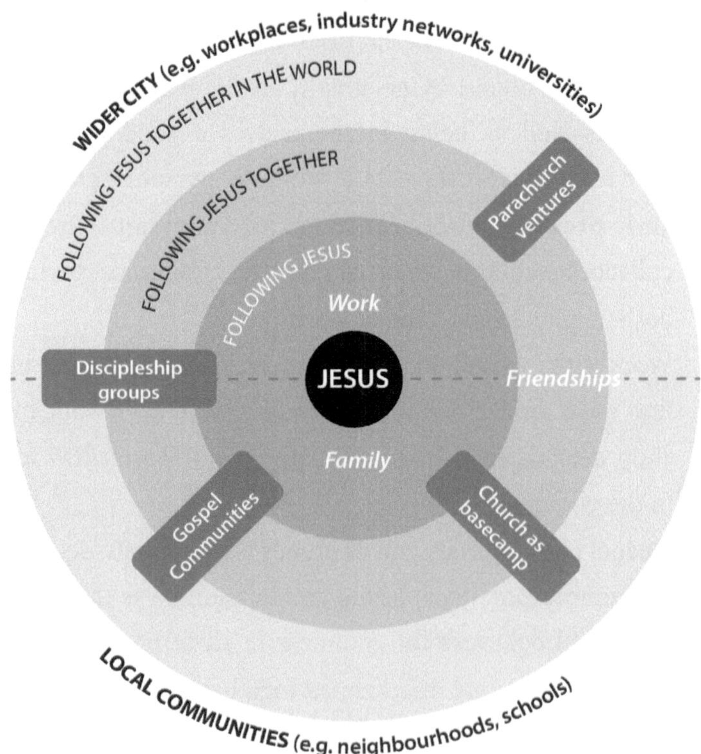

First steps any church could take now

In this chapter, we've wanted to provide a big-picture map of how a church might be organized to promote love. But we haven't tried to outline the smaller steps you might need to take along the way. Every church will have to work out how best to introduce change in its own circumstances.

This said, we think that almost any church could introduce discipleship groups (and indeed, almost any individual could just invite some others to start a discipleship group). In most churches, these won't compete with existing structures, and they can immediately bring some benefits.

Similarly, the four habits we outlined in the gospel community section could be introduced into at least some existing Bible studies over one or two years. Together, these could have a significant impact on the culture of a church: people can taste some of the benefits of a gospel community before they're taught any new theology of church and the Christian life.

Conclusion

One way to think of this book is as part of a philosophy of ministry, or to use Tim Keller's more recent language, a theological vision.[36] A theological vision isn't just raw theology (e.g. four views on ecclesiology), nor is it just a list of prescribed actions (e.g. four steps to growing a church). Rather, a theological vision gives us a set of questions to ask

---

[36] Keller, *Center Church: doing balanced, gospel-centered ministry in your city* (Grand Rapids: Zondervan, 2012).

that help us contemplate carefully and then move to the point of action. "What's the loving thing to do, given what we know from Scripture and what we notice about our current circumstances? What does it mean to hear Jesus's words and do them (Matthew 7:24) *right here and now*?"[37]

Of course, this book is focused on social architecture, so it's only a small portion of what would add up to a theological vision. Social architecture isn't a silver bullet. A more thorough theological vision would need to include such things as God's forgiveness, and how our own lives should be marked by forgiving others; it would discuss the Christian life in light of suffering; it would give a larger account of living within a culture; it would explore the role of work, and how to raise families; it would articulate a fuller doctrine of church and of God's word and of teaching. Our hopes for this book have been more modest.

All this to say, if you end up trying some of our suggestions in your church, it's probably because you already shared a lot of the unstated presuppositions in our theological vision. And presumably you're persuaded that:

- certain kinds of love are desirable in the Christian life and in the church;
- some love is promoted by structures;
- some key aspects of love aren't present in either our Christian or secular cultures;

---

[37] We're indebted here to O'Donovan, "Christian Moral Reasoning," in *New dictionary of Christian ethics and pastoral theology* (eds. Atkinson and Field; Leicester: IVP, 1995). O'Donovan suggests there are two steps to moral reasoning: first, a reflective or descriptive step, where you describe the world (or set of circumstances) in which you need to act; second, a deliberative step, where you think towards action.

- the suggestions we make could go some way to enabling desirable kinds of love.

On our part, formulating these suggested structures has required three distinct kinds of thinking.[38] First, we've read and reflected on Scripture: what God says about his character, his deeds, and his world, and about the kinds of love he desires among his people.

Second, we've observed the world: we've paid attention to how people in general tick, as well as to some of the quirks of our own secular and Christian culture and circumstances. Our observations are inevitably coloured by the fact that we're evangelicals in Sydney, but we hope that some of what we've noticed also pertains to cities in general and to practices that are common in Western Protestant churches. We've also tried to acknowledge that our observations are anecdotal: we haven't commissioned or conducted any formal studies. Indeed, that's a next step for us, and a likely next step for churches who are attracted to some of our ideas. In an appendix to this book, we've provided a short questionnaire that we hope might be useful.

Finally, this book has required imagination. Given what Scripture says, and given the observation that certain church practices don't seem to be very effective, what kind of structures can we imagine that *would* work better?[39]

---

[38] For a fuller account of and defence of these kinds of thinking, see the Groundwork Everyday course *Love and Wisdom*, chapters 7–8, 'Bringing life to the Scriptures'.

[39] Some of our 'imagination' has been informed (sometimes painfully) by our experience. For example, our experience — rather than our imagination — taught us that it was easy to get to know other parents at our children's primary school, but almost impossible to include non-parents into that social circle. Similarly, we've noticed that it's very difficult to have more than two regular, weekly structures in a church. And so on.

Because of this, we're bound to have said things that are irrelevant or even injurious to your church — either because we've made a mistake, or because your circumstances are very different from ours. Accordingly, we'd welcome your feedback, particularly if you've tried to implement some of our suggestions. We're keen to update this book to make it as useful as possible to real church leaders.

Appendix: A survey of your church's discipleship and mission

It's often hard for leaders to accurately assess the kinds of love that are present in a church: we can't know everything that's going on, and the stories we do hear may not be representative of the whole. One way to get a clearer picture of our church's love might be to conduct a survey. We've put together some questions that we think might help, together with some notes to explain *why* we think they're useful.

We should acknowledge that these questions are consistent with the 'philosophy of ministry' or 'theological vision' reflected in this book. So it isn't a survey that analyses church health in a general or abstract way, but church health as we've envisioned it. For example, we ask the question, "Have you had any meaningful conversations with another believer about some aspect of following Jesus?" Embedded in this is the belief that meaningful conversations among Christians are important. The survey will be useful to you to the extent that you agree with our theological vision.

You can download an electronic version of this survey at http://bit.ly/olicsurvey

You can edit it according to your needs, and either print it out or use Google Forms to administer it online.

Notes

1. *"In the last month, have you done* x*?"*

There are a number of questions that ask what people have done in the last month. We're not attempting to discern how people *feel about* or *perceive* church health in general; we're more interested in whether certain concrete loving practices are present. The last month seems like a reasonable timeframe to ask about, both (a) because most of us can probably remember back that far, and (b) these practices should be fairly frequent in the Christian life.

In asking just about the last month, the survey will provide a snapshot of the whole church, rather than a detailed account of any individual's life. That is, if I didn't have anyone from church in my home in the last month, there may be any number of reasons (e.g. illness, a new baby, a holiday, a new job, a too-small apartment). But if almost no one had opened their home, it would provide useful information about the church culture.

In addition, we haven't asked anything about church structures. We think the best way to determine how effective church structures are is to ask about particular habits or practices: again, we're more interested in *results* (what actually happens) than *processes* (what we think *should* happen if we adopt a certain structure). So we don't ask, "Do you find your small group encouraging?" but rather, "Have you had an encouraging conversation?"

2. *"Have you had a conversation about* x*?"*

We're assuming that concrete conversations about specific topics are a good indicator that conversations are happening more generally. As well as being one of our key elements of discipleship and mission, conversations may work as a kind of proxy for good-quality friendships.

3. *"Have you had a conversation with another believer, other than a member of church staff?"*

There are important questions we could ask about interactions between church members and staff, but here we're primarily focused on how church members interact with each other and the world around them. That is, we're less interested in direct acts of love performed by staff, and more interested in the culture of love across the whole church.

4. *"...in your church"*

Because this is a survey about church health, we're primarily interested in the kinds of love Christians are expressing and receiving *in their local church*. As we've said in the book, we hope Christian love goes *beyond* the church, too, but we should expect the experience of love *at least* within the church.

Questionnaire

1. In the last month, have you had a meaningful conversation about your work life with someone from church, other than a staff member?
   By 'meaningful', we're indicating the kind of conversation where the details of your work were discussed, including such things as opportunities for you to do good, or temptations to do ill.

   ☐ Yes ☐ No

2. In the last month, have you had a meaningful conversation about the struggles or joys of your particular life-stage with someone in church, other than a staff member?

   ☐ Yes ☐ No

3. If you're married, are you content in your marriage?

   ☐ Yes ☐ No

   If not, have you talked about this with anyone in your church?

   ☐ Yes ☐ No

4. Is there someone younger or older in your church whom you're encouraging or being encouraged by?

   ☐ Yes ☐ No

   If so, do you interact with them often enough to see what their family life looks like?

   ☐ Yes ☐ No

5. In the last month, have you had anyone in your church over for a meal in your house?

   ☐ Yes ☐ No

6. In the last month, have you spent time socially with Christians and non-Christians together?

☐ Yes ☐ No

7. In the last month, outside formal structures (like Bible studies or Sunday gatherings), have you had a conversation with someone at church about some aspect of Scripture?

☐ Yes ☐ No

8. In the last month, have you had a conversation with an unbeliever about something meaningful or personal or 'deep'?
For example, work struggles, relationships, parenting, politics, etc.

☐ Yes ☐ No

If so, did that conversation include any mention of Jesus?

☐ Yes ☐ No

9. In the last month, have you loved someone in a sacrificial way, or been a recipient of such love yourself?
For example: making a meal for a sick person, doing some gardening or painting at someone else's place, helping someone move house, visiting a shut-in or a 'difficult person', giving a lift to the airport, paying a bill, doing some babysitting, etc.

☐ Yes ☐ No

10. Are you struggling with a lack of self-control in some area of life?
Including but not limited to food (overeating or obsessive 'healthy' eating), excessive spending, pornography, alcohol, keeping your house tidy, exercise, gossip, playing computer games, watching TV, checking Facebook.

☐ Yes ☐ No

If so, have you talked about this with anyone in your church?

☐ Yes ☐ No

www.ingramcontent.com/pod-product-compliance
Ingram Content Group UK Ltd.
Pitfield, Milton Keynes, MK11 3LW, UK
UKHW041933190726
13854UKWH00004B/1559